The Convert's Guide to Roman Catholicism

Your First Year in the Church

Keith Nester

Acknowledgements:

Proofread by Estelle Ruchniewski
Edited by Jane Cavolina
Formatted by Irena Kalcheva
Cover photo by Estelle Nester
Cover design by Devin Schadt

This book was written at the Community
of St. John, Princeville IL and the
home of Greg and Sandi Hansen.
Thank you for your hospitality.

All Bible references are taken from the New
Revised Standard Version Catholic Edition
except those indicated by * which come from
the Revised Standard Version Catholic Edition

ISBN: 9781700289773

To Estelle, the love of my life. Thank you for always believing in me.

This book would not exist without you. I am so proud to be your husband.

You are God's great gift to me.

Contents

Here's the deal:

The point of this book is not my conversion story, but rather it is a guide for those who, like me, have recently converted to the Catholic Church (or are preparing to do so). I write through my own experience. Other people's perspectives will undoubtedly be different, but I am hoping these ideas will be useful to everyone. This is not an apologetics book (fancy Catholic and Protestant word for "defense"). I am in no way qualified to write an apologetics book. I am not that smart. There are already a ton of great apologetics resources out there. I am a total nerd for all that stuff, but that was not the direction God led me. This book contains some basic things that you may need as you make the transition into Catholicism, but I'll leave all the heavy lifting to the guys at Catholic Answers.

Introduction

October 14, 2018, was the day I knew this book had to happen. It was a Sunday. I was sitting next to my wife, Estelle, on a bus headed for Split, Croatia. We were finishing an eight day pilgrimage (fancy Catholic word for "trip") to a small village in Bosnia where some people claim they have been receiving messages from the Virgin Mary. I know, it sounds weird, but don't freak out. We will cover this topic later. We were two thirds of the way through the three-hour trip when we all began to pray the Chaplet of Divine Mercy. As we prayed, something I cannot explain happened. I pulled out my phone and started typing into the Notes app. I turned to my wife and showed her the note I had just typed. The look on her face said, *What the heck are you doing. We're supposed to be praying?* "This is the title of the book I am supposed to write," I said to her. *"The Convert's Guide to Roman Catholicism: Your First Year in the Church."*

Her eyes widened and her jaw dropped. Estelle had been waiting and praying for months for God to speak to us, especially on this trip, which was almost over. The previous night, she had an incredible encounter with a priest during confession, which encouraged her to keep waiting and trusting in God. Could this be part of the answer? A week earlier we had arrived in Croatia. It was October 8, 2018, my one-year anniversary as a Roman Catholic.

Prior to my conversion, I had worked in full-time professional ministry for twenty-two years in various capacities and denominations. The last position I held was in a United Methodist Church, where I served as Pastor to Youth and Mission for six years. That title scratched the surface of what I actually did, but let's just say I was the second in command at a relatively large and very busy church. I preached every other Sunday to around seven hundred people and every Wednesday night to a hundred or so students. I loved it. Youth ministry was what I was mostly known for in my twenties, but I had also done much in worship, missions, and camping. In ministry, I was a jack-of-all-trades. I could do a funeral service for someone in the morning and then take a dodgeball to the face a couple hours later at youth group. I also did a lot of fund-raising as well as preparing and leading our mission trips to Haiti. I had to be good at running lots of programs and dealing with all types of people. The position was very demanding, but also a lot of fun. I loved serving God and my church family.

I didn't want to admit it growing up, but I was destined to be in ministry. My dad was a United Methodist pastor for forty years and the most formative moments of my life revolved around my faith. My parents never pushed me into ministry, but childhood experiences at church camp shaped who I would become. As a young adult, I felt the call to ministry and was offered a job as a youth pastor serving under my friend Craig. I had been to camp with Craig every summer since I was ten.

Ministry became my world. Estelle and our three kids were not exactly the typical pastor's family, but we loved the church. Being a youth pastor wasn't just a job; it was our whole identity. When I left all of that behind to convert to Roman Catholicism, it left us with many unanswered questions.

How would we survive?

What could I possibly do at forty-four years old with a degree in religion?

Do I have any useful skills outside of ministry?

Does this mean Estelle will become Catholic?

How will she be affected?

What about the kids?

Would we force them to leave their church too?

How will our families deal with this?

What about our friends?

Most of our relationships are centered around church. How will these relationships be affected?

Where are we supposed to go to church now?

How should I go about telling people about this?

Do I have to become a Facebook Crusader? (This is what I call people who think social media is the best place to broadcast their theological insights and opinions.)

How will I respond when I am challenged by people who oppose my conversion?

Can I really make it as a Catholic?

What if I hate it?

What if I miss being a Protestant?

What if I can't buy into everything the Church teaches?

What about my gifts for ministry?

Will I ever be useful to God if I can't be a pastor anymore?

4

All of these questions, and more, had gone from being hypothetical to very real.

It had been over a year. Estelle had been convinced that surely by then something would have happened to give us direction. Undoubtedly, God would have spoken and told us what was next. Surely all of the questions would have worked themselves out by now. Some had. Some hadn't. A year in, this is what I knew:

Converting to Catholicism was harder than I could've imagined.

And

Converting to Catholicism was more amazing than I could've imagined.

We have learned a lot in our first year. Some things have been awesome. Some things have been disappointing. All of it has helped us grow. We want to share it with you. This book was written to help people do what we did, and although every story is unique, there are some general principles that can guide you and make the transition easier.

So if you're up for an adventure and you can handle a down-to-earth, blunt smart-aleck, and sarcastic tour guide, welcome to your first year in the Catholic Church.

Chapter 1

Why Do People Convert?
Seriously? It's a thing

Newcomer Orientation was always one of my favorite things we did when I was a pastor. The title is exactly correct. This was a time to welcome newcomers into our church and give them an overall explanation of what our church was about and who we were as a church staff. It also gave us the chance to learn what was bringing people to our congregation. We sat around a table in Pastor Craig's office, ate donuts, drank coffee, and listened to people tell us why they wanted to come to our church. As a pastor, it was usually pretty awesome. Hearing people tell you why out of all the churches in the city they chose *yours* (and consequently *you*) for spiritual fulfillment did not stink at all. (Part of me wonders what it would be like to have New*leavers* Parting Shots but who would be crazy enough to handle that?)

The stories we heard in those meetings were diverse and often moving. Some people wound up with us because they recently moved to the area and promised their parents they would join the closest Methodist church. Others heard about our talented worship band, engaging sermons, and great youth programs and just had to check it out. For some people, coming to our church was the result of a conflict they had in their previous church. We would listen to what set them off, and part of the time we would be thinking, *Yes!! We* **are** *the best church in town!* However, if someone had told us they had left multiple churches over conflict, we would usually expect them to eventually leave our church too. I heard many stories from people who described themselves as "ex-Catholics." The story was almost always the same.

> *Raised in the Church but with no personal faith experience or understanding of the Bible.*
>
> *Went through confirmation classes only to be bored to tears.*
>
> *Attended Church on Christmas and Easter and tried to be "a good person" so I could make it to Heaven.*
>
> *A friend invited me to this church and I was blown away by how friendly everyone was. The whole atmosphere was different. People were having fun. The music was amazing. The band played songs I heard on the radio. Even my kids love it here! Children's church and youth group have my kids asking me, "Is it time to go to church yet?" The sermons speak directly to what's going on in my life. The pastor makes the Bible seem relevant to where I am in life. I finally heard the gospel in a way that makes sense to me and I accepted Jesus as my personal Lord and savior! There's so much to do around here to grow and meet other people. This is so much better than the dull boring routine of being Catholic. How do we join?*

This story was very real and personal to me because it's basically the story of my wife, Estelle. Estelle was raised Catholic. She grew up in northeast Philadelphia and went to Catholic school her entire life. She was a good person and had a belief in God, but her faith was not central to her life, and she knew next to nothing about the Bible. She rarely went to church. Shortly after we met, I invited her to the nondenominational church I was attending. It was a great church. Calvary Chapel of Philadelphia is a megachurch (thousands in attendance each week). Pastor Joe, an ex-Catholic, preached "verse by verse" sermons through books of the Bible. He was an incredible teacher and communicator. The music was contemporary and led us in deep, meaningful worship. Estelle was blown away. She had never experienced anything like this. I remember the moment when she turned to me with huge eyes and said, "Thank you for bringing me here." At the end of each service, Pastor Joe invited anyone who wanted to pray and receive Jesus Christ personally to come forward for prayer. Estelle was probably the first one that night. She raced to the front of the auditorium and gave her life to Jesus. For her, everything changed almost immediately. Her faith became real. Her love for Jesus was now the most important thing. Church was now something she couldn't get enough of. She had unapologetically left the Catholic Church behind.

There were some variations, but this is essentially the story I heard dozens of times at Newcomer Orientation. Ex-Catholics were everywhere. But what about ex-Protestants? Are they a thing? We were used to people eventually leaving our church to go to new churches with better bands and bigger buildings, but nobody I knew left to become a Catholic.

Chapter 2

The First One

How did I miss this?

In 1998, my little youth group was starting to grow. What had previously been a small gathering of students was becoming one of the largest youth services of its kind in the state of Iowa. With a full scale rock band, and nearly three hundred students each week, exciting things were happening at our little church in Iowa. Believe it or not, something happened during the process of growing this youth group that first opened my eyes to the Catholic Church. It was beyond exciting. My first Wednesday night meeting in 1995 had about a dozen students. It was great. I loved those kids. More than anything, I wanted to see them grow in their love of God and for each other. I wasn't much older than some of them, but I took on sort of a big brother role. I would spend time hanging out with them at the mall. I would go to their school activities and celebrate their achievements. If they had any problems, I would offer myself as a person for them to talk to. We had activities, trips, and service projects almost weekly. It was important for the congregation and for the parents of these students to see these kids active and busy in the life of the church. Each week I would plan our Wednesday night youth group time with the hopes that the games, sermon, and small group times would help these kids grow. We were not without our fair share of drama and issues, but all in all, our little group was pretty awesome. However, I felt the pressure to see it grow. *Why aren't more kids coming?* I used to wonder. *What's wrong with me?* There were other youth groups in town that had much larger attendance, and our students would sometimes ask me why we didn't do some of the things they did. I wanted to see growth, but I really didn't know how to make that happen. What I did know was that some things needed to change.

In 1997, I attended an event called Acquire the Fire at an arena in Des Moines. It blew me away. Acquire the Fire was produced by a ministry named "Teen Mania," led by Ron Luce. Ron was a hero to me. He understood the importance of reaching "this generation" (fancy youth ministry name for "kids in high school") with the gospel and challenging them to spiritual greatness. His methods were right up my alley. Excitement, music, high energy messages, even pyrotechnics! All of the stuff we were missing. No wonder our kids were bored and weren't bringing their friends. We needed to give them something they could be proud of, not the typical run-of-the-mill youth group with stupid crowd breakers (youth-group name for "ridiculous activity you do in the beginning of the meeting"), watered-down sermons, and pointless activities. I left that conference on a mission. We had to ditch our youth group and make something awesome . . . for Jesus."

There was work to do. We had to start a band (luckily, I was a musician). We needed a more exciting environment than the church sanctuary, time to remodel the "fellowship hall" (church name for "big room with tables and chairs connected to a kitchen"). Next, we needed a catchy name. A cool ministry needs a cool name. You can't just call it "youth group". Our church was on Pine Street. One of the students wrote "Pine Street High," on my office door one day. I thought that was perfect! *Pine Street High* would be our new name. Now we needed a logo. That's right, a logo. After all, you have to have something cool to put on T-shirts, stickers, and banners.

I looked through the Yellow Pages (remember, this was 1998) to find a graphic designer who could make something amazing. I wanted everything about our new identity and ministry to be the best. "How to Have a World-Class Youth Ministry" was the name of the presentation Ron Luce taught at the youth pastor breakout session of Acquire the Fire. I wanted to follow everything he said to the letter. That meant no "Design a Logo" contest at my church. I was going to hire a professional. Ron Luce told us so!

The first person I called was a woman who got more than she bargained for when she answered the phone. I told her what I was looking for and gave her way too much information. She said, "I can't help you, but I know the perfect person. His name is Devin Schadt. He is an amazing designer and he would be interested in this type of thing." I called him right away. Devin sounded cool over the phone. He was excited to hear about my youth ministry and wanted to help. He sounded like a guy who loved Jesus and believed in reaching kids. *Maybe I could recruit him to volunteer on Wednesday nights*, I thought. Devin agreed to come up with some ideas and meet me at his home. I couldn't wait to see what he came up with, and meet him face-to-face.

The night Devin agreed to meet was Estelle and my wedding anniversary. I promised Estelle I would be back quickly. I drove a couple of miles into an older neighborhood in the center of town to Devin's house. As I approached the front door, I was a little thrown off by the statues near the porch. Maybe I was at the wrong place? *Why would this guy have statues of the Virgin Mary and some other guy in his front yard? Maybe this was his grandmother's house or something? Wait, why would he live with his grandmother?*

I knocked on the door not knowing what I was in for. When Devin answered, I was immediately welcomed with a warm greeting into a house I can only describe as slightly less Catholic-looking than the Sistine Chapel. There were paintings of Jesus, Mary, and other Catholic-looking people everywhere. There were even more statues. There was a bowl filled with water next to the front door. The place was beautiful and immaculate. There was no TV. Nothing decorated this incredible house other than things that must have been either stolen from a European museum or gleaned from a Catholic Church going-out-of-business sale.

We sat at the dining-room table and Devin asked me to tell him more about our church and youth ministry. As I explained our plans and "vision" (fancy church word for "idea"), he became very excited and seemed to really believe in what I was saying. He opened a folder containing some rough ideas for a logo he'd made after our phone conversation. I was in love with the very first one. This guy had unbelievable talent. Man, if only I could recruit him!

"This is all amazing, Devin, but before I leave I just have to ask you something," I said.

"Sure, what is it?" he replied.

"I don't mean to be disrespectful . . ."

"Yeah?"

"But what's with all this Catholic stuff? You seem like an 'on fire' (fancy evangelical word for "serious or passionate") Christian."

Devin laughed loudly and said, "I am very on fire (Devin could speak Christianese) for Jesus and I am that way *because* I am Catholic."

What went through my mind next was a mixture of two things. First, I thought, *If this guy really loves Jesus, I can convert him easily by showing him some Scripture that demonstrates where and why the Catholics do not follow the Bible, or Jesus, in favor of man-made traditions. If he really wants Jesus, he will leave all this superstitious garbage behind once I show him a couple of verses. Secondly, I thought, I better not offend this guy because he is designing my logo and I don't want to make him mad."

All of this while keeping in mind Estelle was waiting for me to get home to celebrate our anniversary. I decided to ask him the most direct but revealing question I could think of: "Devin, when were you saved?"

This was a trick question. I was asking a question that meant different things to different people. I wanted to see how a Catholic would answer. I knew the correct (or evangelical) answer dealt with the specific time I asked Jesus into my heart to be my personal Lord and Savior. I didn't think Catholics believed anything like that.

Devin then proceeded to tell me about his life and his faith. (He has written his own books about that. I recommend them). He told me how at one point he had abandoned God altogether, but through the sacraments (*what?*) and the Church (*which one?*), he had been given tremendous grace by God and has dedicated his life to serving God. (*Who is this guy?*)

He described his faith and relationship with Jesus in a way that was so inspiring, and in some bizarre way, on such a different level than anything I was familiar with that I was speechless. I had never seen or heard any Catholic talk like this. I still wanted to see how he would react to some of the verses I had in mind that I thought could strip him of his Catholicism, but those conversations would have to come later (and they did . . . a lot!), but thankfully Devin's wife, Kim, called down from upstairs, "You guys! It's Keith's anniversary. He needs to go *home!*"

"Oh, crap!!!!" I have to go!!!

Devin said, "Keith, before you leave, let me give you something to watch that might be interesting." He handed me a VHS tape with a grainy photo of a guy who looked like my dad shaking hands with the pope. It was called *The Scott Hahn Conversion Story*. "This guy was like you, only worse, and he became Catholic," Devin said. We both laughed loudly and then I left.

When I arrived home, I said, "Honey, you aren't going to believe this."

"OK, tell me about it . . . hey great, you rented a movie for us to watch for our anniversary!"

"Not exactly," I replied.

Scott Hahn is a name that, as a convert, you need to be familiar with. He has helped untold multitudes of people find their way into the Catholic faith. He is a convert to the faith from a perspective of Protestantism that isn't just *non*-Catholic but decidedly *anti*-Catholic. It's true that all Protestants oppose at least some of the doctrines of the Catholic faith (most notably those doctrines surrounding the authority of the pope), but there are certain groups of Protestants that oppose the Catholic Church as evil, unchristian, and even satanic in nature. Most of the people I know who hold this view aren't ready to say that individual Catholics are evil, but they will certainly say that the institution of the Catholic Church is, and has always been.

Scott Hahn was one of those guys. If you haven't heard or read his conversion story, you should definitely check it out. Because I knew Scott Hahn's type of thinking (I agreed with much of what he believed), I was very curious how a guy like him could become a Catholic. *He was a pastor! What was he thinking?* Watching Scott's talk was life changing. Here was a man who knew the Bible backward and forward, had a passionate relationship with Jesus, was educated in a top seminary, and had everything to lose by becoming a Catholic, and he did it anyway. *Why? Was he a fluke? Were there others like him?* These questions needed answers. Devin and I would continue to get together and talk (and sometimes yell), theology. It seems as if I had made it my mission to convert him out of the Catholic Church, and he made it his mission to convert me into it.

It was like Pandora's Box had been opened and there was no stopping it. Books and magazines were flying at me from every direction. I learned quickly that Scott Hahn was not alone in his discoveries. Devin gave me other books—*Born Fundamentalist, Born Again Catholic* and *The Spirit of Catholicism*, to name a few. Apologetics manuals designed to refute the stock Protestant objections were piling up on my desk. These works were filled with quotes from the Church

Fathers (early Christian leaders) and other people from history that I had heard about in college and seminary. A man named Marcus Grodi is a former Protestant minister who runs an organization called The Coming Home Network, which exists to provide support and encouragement to people (and especially pastors) of all denominations who were leaving behind their objections, traditions, and even careers to become Catholic. Each week his program *The Journey Home* tells the story of another convert's journey to the Roman Catholic Church. I watched many episodes. What was striking to me is what they were saying about what drew them to Catholicism, but also what they weren't saying.

In Newcomer Orientation, I never heard anyone leave the Catholic Church because they had studied the Scripture and the history of the Church and became convinced that the United Methodist Church (or any other Protestant church) was the true church, or even the closest to the church of Jesus and his apostles. I never heard anyone say they were leaving Catholicism because of doctrinal issues. I never heard anyone say they were drawn to our church because of some great theological revelation. Most of the people leaving the Church and coming to us were coming for reasons such as conflict with the Church, an issue with their marriage, or they were just bored and thought our church was more fun.

"I don't like the music," "I'm bored," "I'm sick of the same old thing," "the priest didn't greet me when I saw him in public," "my kids hate going to church so I need to find one they enjoy," "the Church didn't give me what I wanted," "the Church doesn't accept my new marriage as valid," "the Protestant church across town has a better preacher, etc."

I've heard these reasons (except the one about marriage) from people leaving Protestant churches for other Protestant churches too.

There are, of course, other variants, but by and large these were the main reasons.

Mother Angelica (look her up on YouTube) once said, "The Catholics get the *best* Protestants and the Protestants get the *worst* Catholics." Even when I was a pastor I thought that was pretty funny. Her point was, if you examine the reasons people convert from Catholicism to Protestantism, and vice versa, what you find is people are either running away from, or running to, the historic, ancient, and apostolic teaching of the Christian faith. It's just that they don't always recognize that for what it is. What draws people to Catholicism is not the same thing that draws others away. In my limited experience, what I have seen is that most people are drawn to Catholicism for doctrinal and historical reasons. Most people are drawn away for personal ones.

So what draws people to Catholicism? Is everyone who converts to Catholicism doing so because of some holy quest to discover the one true Church? Hardly! There are plenty of people joining the Catholic Church so they can appease someone (usually their future in-laws). I'm not talking about that. I'm talking about people who are serious about their faith, and are making the decision to convert because of their love for Jesus. Being a "member" of a church isn't the same thing as being in deep relationship with Jesus. People can join a church, but the reasons why are very important. God knows that just because someone's name is on an official church membership roll, that doesn't mean they have an authentic faith. That's not a Catholic or Protestant problem; it's a *human* problem. Let's be real about this. What has drawn you to convert? That's a huge question for converts to answer, because if you don't know why you are doing this, then how will you stick with it when it becomes difficult? How will you answer those people in your life who will want to know why? What will you say when you are challenged? Will you stick with it when you become disappointed in some aspect of your new church experience?

I want to encourage you to stop right now and take some time to develop your answers to the following questions:

1. Why do I want to become Catholic?
2. What are three aspects of Roman Catholicism that I believe are not present in other churches?
3. Am I willing to obey the Church's teaching no matter what it means for my life?

These are tough but important questions. Hopefully this book will not only help you answer them for yourself but give you the encouragement you need to make it through the first year.

Chapter 3

How Not to Have a Holy War

Coming out as a Catholic

This chapter is about how you go about telling people you are converting. More importantly, how *not* to go about telling people you are converting. I remember when one of my best friends became a Calvinist. We went to church together and were very close. We helped each other immensely in our Christian faith as young men. Our conversations were fruitful but usually pretty shallow in terms of our faith or any kind of doctrine. That was fine by me, but it all changed one night. My friend came to an overnight event I had brought some students to, and informed me that he had discovered the truth about the "doctrines of grace". I had no idea what he was talking about, but the next thing I knew he had me cornered in a gymnasium and wouldn't stop talking about how God had predestined everyone's eternal salvation or damnation and there was nothing anybody could do about it. For the next two years it was all he talked about with me. Five-Point Calvinism, R. C. Sproul, and predestination dominated our conversations. I read some of the books he gave me and thought, *OK, whatever,*

I don't believe that. Let's move on. Over time he chilled out a bit and though his beliefs have remained, he once apologized to me for his time in the "cage phase." (He remains a great friend and pastor to this day).

The "cage phase" refers to the first two years someone is a Calvinist and needs to be locked in a cage because they will drive all their friends crazy with their new theology. I thought it was hilarious that this was a term some Calvinists created and applied to themselves. The truth is, the cage phase could also be applied to anyone (including us new Catholic converts) if we don't play our cards right.

I am not suggesting that new converts need to be secretive or undercover. What I am suggesting is that new converts need to be wise, loving, and above all, filled with grace. Maybe you're like that naturally. I am not. When I announced my conversion to Roman Catholicism to my church, I had to write a resignation letter. The letter was rejected by my senior pastor and church board because they deemed it harmful. Maybe they were right. Maybe they were just doing damage control. Either way, I had to rewrite it and make it more grace filled and softer in tone. Don't get me wrong. I love my old church. I was not mad at them. I did not want to hurt them in any way. It's just that in my newfound faith, I had conveyed my desire to become Catholic in a way that was self-righteous, condescending, and prideful. While all of it was true, much of what I wrote was unhelpful. My revised version contained a somewhat softer tone and alluded to the fact that I had simply sensed a deeper calling to the Roman Catholic Church and had decided to pursue it. Sometimes I feel like I still should've sent the first letter, but I know that would not have been smart. This type of information is best shared in private conversations between people who care about each other, not statements or announcements.

Here are my suggestions as you come out as a Catholic.

1. No Facebook posts.

You can use Facebook to share what's going on in your life, but for everyone's sake (including yours) do not post a message announcing your conversion. People often feel like they have to leave comments whether they agree or disagree. You don't want to spend your time overanalyzing comments, reactions, or the lack of reactions from your Facebook friends. People tend to say things online they normally wouldn't say in person, not to mention what can happen when arguments start in the comment section between your Facebook friends who may not even know each other. Eventually, your world will find out you've converted and then you can post relevant things, but don't use Facebook (or other social media platforms) to announce it.

2. Never assume that people will be against you. Do not get defensive.

It's natural for you to be a bit defensive at first. Try not to assume how anyone will react. Some of the people you would expect to freak out the most may surprise you. If you act defensive, you may cause unnecessary conflict. Give people the benefit of the doubt. Most of them will be nice, even if they don't get it. I certainly have had plenty of tough conversations with people about my conversion, but I have also had some great words of encouragement even from non-Catholics. People who love you will want what's best for you. Even if they don't understand your Catholicism, they still may be happy for you. Give people a chance. Don't have a chip on your shoulder.

3. Welcome questions and conversations.

I greatly appreciate it when someone asks me about my conversion—even when I know they disapprove. What was tough was when people talked *about* me rather than *to* me. If someone cares enough about you to ask you about your conversion, respond with gratitude. Be open. Answer questions and thank them for talking to you about it. Let them know they can always talk to you about their questions or concerns. You may be surprised at the doors that open. It's been awesome to hear from old friends or acquaintances who are curious about why I converted. Be the kind of person who is approachable and available. If someone wants to talk, set some time aside for them. These are conversations best had in person, although that's not always possible. When someone sends a text or email, or hits you up on social media, suggest getting together. It's important to hear tone and convey body language when having these types of conversations. Try to make that happen when you can. It communicates value and love to people.

4. Do not speak negatively of Protestants.

Your conversion does not make you better than anyone else. You have not earned the right to start bashing anyone, especially Protestants. When people convert, there can be a tendency to poke holes in the position they once held. There are many reasons why that's a bad idea, but for starters, it's not very loving. Talking negatively about Protestants will also ruin your opportunity to share your story. No one will want to talk to you if they feel like you'll be argumentative or threatening. Besides, you *were* a Protestant. You were there. You had to go through a process to get to where you are. Allow people to be where they are as well. If you start putting people on the defensive, they will build a wall to the message you bring. Speaking negatively about others is never the way to go. Your conversion story needs to be much more about what you came to, rather than what you left behind.

5. Make your first priority your own spiritual health.

Your conversion needs to be more about your own holiness rather than your conversion. I know that may sound contradictory, but it's actually the point. If becoming Catholic doesn't make you more like Jesus, then you are doing it wrong. By growing closer to God, you will be led by the Spirit in all things, including how to tell your world that you are a Catholic. Don't be obsessed with letting everyone know you are a Catholic. Be obsessed with becoming more like Jesus. Remember what Jesus said: [3] "Why do you see the speck in your neighbor's eye, but do not notice the log in your own eye?[4] Or how can you say to your neighbor, 'Let me take the speck out of your eye,' while the log is in your own eye?[5] You hypocrite, first take the log out of your own eye, and then you will see clearly to take the speck out of your neighbor's eye." (Matthew 7:3–5).

Holiness and love for God and neighbor are your top priority, and will be the fruit of your Catholicism. Focus on becoming the best Christian you can be, and people will want to know more.

6. Prepare for people to treat you like you just died. Develop a thick skin and a soft heart.

Unfortunately, there will be some people in your life who will struggle with your conversion. The severity of that struggle depends on many factors, but I can promise you, not everybody will understand. I've had good friends say hurtful things about me without ever talking to me directly. I've had other people, who were once very close to me, completely stop talking to me. It's all part of the deal when you convert, and others have had it much worse, but it's something you have to be ready for. It's tough, but I have taken comfort in the fact that whenever people speak evil of me for the sake of my faith, Jesus says I am blessed (Matthew 5:11–12). Try to understand that some people are probably genuinely concerned about your soul. They think you have gone crazy. Give them grace. Do not return their negativity with more negativity. Instead, show them love.

This is part of the cross we bear as converts. Take it up and follow Jesus. Eventually things have a way of working themselves out. If those relationships were really that strong, people will learn to accept you. Especially if you remain humble. For many people, their negative reaction to your conversion is much more about them than you. Perhaps they had a bad experience with the Catholic Church? Maybe they believe things that aren't true about Catholic doctrine. I certainly did! Try not to take their rejection of your Catholicism personally. Remember the words of St. Paul, in Romans 12:18: "If it is possible, so far as it depends on you, live peaceably with all." If people try to hurt you, respond with grace (or not at all). When people attack you, be humble. It's not your job to fight, but you do need a thick skin. Let your Catholic faith be a shield, not a sword. God has a way of dealing with these types of situations. Leave the offense to God.

7. Do not try to convert everyone who asks you about your conversion.

Try to resist the urge to tell everyone who talks to you about your conversion that they must become Catholic too. There will be opportunities for those types of conversations, but if you come at everyone with guns blazing, they will shut you down and never want to talk to you about your faith. Your conversion will make them think about themselves. You don't need to force it. When people feel like they can trust you, they will eventually make their way to you. Create an open environment for people to talk to you about your conversion and they will undoubtedly think about it for themselves in due time. It's not your job to make them Catholic. It's your job to be the instrument of Jesus. Perhaps God will use you to bring about conversions. Perhaps God will use you to plant the seed. Be open and obedient, but also wise and humble. Seeds will be planted that may take years to grow. Be patient but ready.

8. Do not insist on imposing your Catholicism on your family and friends when you are in their homes.

Because I was a pastor for so many years, I am often asked to pray before meals when I am with family or friends. If I'm in my home, I always make the sign of the cross and pray, "Bless us, O Lord, and these Thy gifts . . . ," the standard prayer before meals (you'll learn it). If I'm in the home of someone who is not Catholic, I try to gauge the environment to see if a typical

Catholic prayer is the way to go. Sometimes it is, sometimes it isn't. When you're in someone else's home, respect who they are. Don't make a big production out of your Catholicism and try to get everyone to do what you do. That only adds to false ideas that Catholics are wacko and superstitious. When they come to your house, or if you are out to eat, that's a different story. They should respect you in your house just like you respect them in theirs. Never turn your Catholicism into a show for other people. Remember Jesus' words about practicing your faith to be seen by others (Matthew 6:5). If you try to make everyone conform to the way you pray or eat then you run the risk of making a spectacle of yourself.

9. Recognize that how you live is way more important than what you say.

This is the most important idea of all. If all that people know about your conversion is what they hear from you, then that's a problem. People need to see how your becoming a Catholic has made you more like Jesus. The most effective way to share your newfound Catholic faith is by being a joy-filled, devoted, humble, generous, graceful, loving, and strong follower of Jesus. When people see how your Catholicism has enhanced your discipleship it will dispel any fears that you have somehow lost your faith. One of my good friends (who no longer talks to me) said of me, "I don't know why Keith wants to go backward in his faith into man-made religion." As much as that stung, I realized that since I converted we have had exactly zero conversations. This person hasn't experienced me as a Catholic, or had any contact with me. How can this person judge me? I can only pray that one day our friendship will be rekindled and we can spend some time together. Lord willing, this person would have a different opinion of the direction my faith has taken me—provided that I can live out my faith in a way that brings honor to Christ. If people hear you talk about how amazing Catholicism is, but see no evidence in your life of a greater conversion to Christ, then it would be better for you to stop talking.

10. Cover everything you do and say in prayer.

It goes without saying that in all things, you must become a person of prayer. Pray for those with whom you will share your faith. Pray for those who hear about your conversion and speak evil. Pray for those to whom God will send you. Pray that every time you say or do anything to show your conversion to others, that God will fill you with his Spirit. Pray that you will be a faithful witness to Christ. Pray for those with "ears to hear" to be brought into your path. And most importantly, pray that your heart would be more transformed into the likeness of Jesus.

This journey you've begun will ask more from you than you can imagine. Sacrifices will be made. Lives will be changed. There will be some difficult days ahead for you, but there will also be days filled with unspeakable joy.

Pray! Pray! Pray!

Chapter 4

Finding a Local Church
*What you need to know, what you need
to do, what you need to not do*

What You Need to Know

Go to Mass every Sunday.

One of the precepts (rules) of the Catholic faith is that all
Catholics are obligated to attend Mass every Sunday and on
Holy Days of Obligation. Going to church *every* Sunday may or
may not be something you're used to. For me, it was certainly
the routine (I worked there, remember), but on weeks off,
when traveling I didn't always insist we attend church. Many
Christians (Protestant and Catholic alike) stink at going to
church. The reasons and excuses are endless, but at the end of
the day, as Catholics, we must recognize that we must go. Does
that seem weird to you? Does it feel strange for the Church to
tell you that willfully skipping Mass without a valid reason is a
serious sin? When I was a pastor, if we told people it was a sin
to willfully skip church we would have been laughed at. Why

the obligation? Because Sunday Mass is both the memorial of what Christ has done for us on the Cross and the celebration of his Resurrection. The Church guides us through the calendar in seasons, like Lent and Advent, that are intrinsically tied to our faith as Christians. If we skip weeks, then we fail to complete the journey with the Church toward Christ. But what if you just don't feel like going? You must remember that the Mass is not for you. The Mass is not a "service" designed to help you in your life or make you feel a certain way (although it does both). The Mass is not a concert or a classroom. The Mass is not a social hour. The Mass is ultimately for God. The Mass is where Heaven and Earth meet as the sacrifice of Calvary is made present on the altar. How can we obey the Lord's command to "Do this in memory of me" (Luke 22:19) if we fail to show up? No matter what the frequency of your church attendance was in the past, as a Catholic, you must make weekly Sunday Mass attendance absolutely nonnegotiable. This doesn't have to be an impossible request. The Church makes it very easy to fulfill this obligation. There are likely plenty of Masses (depending on where you live) to attend at all different times. Another thing to consider is that attending Mass on Saturday evening fulfills your Sunday obligation. You can do this! You just have to make it a priority and work at it when you are out of your normal routine.

In addition to the weekly Sunday obligation there are a few other days where Mass attendance is required. Holy Days of Obligation mark special celebrations when the faithful must gather for Mass. Holy Days of Obligation vary from country to country, and sometimes a Sunday obligation will also fulfill a Holy Day of Obligation. The best thing to do is look on a Church calendar and make a plan for how you will fulfill your obligation. Try not to worry too much about it. It sounds harder than it is. For example, in the United States in 2019 there are/were only six non-Sundays that are Holy Days of Obligation:

> **January 1:** Solemnity of Mary, the Holy Mother of God
> **May 30:** Ascension of the Lord
> **August 15:** Solemnity of the Assumption of the Blessed Virgin Mary
> **November 1:** All Saints' Day
> **December 8:** The Feast of the Immaculate Conception.
> **December 25:** The Nativity of the Lord

Make these days part of your year. You'll be glad you did.

Understand the liturgical year.

In the history of God's people, certain events were celebrated yearly. The Jews had seven required feasts, according to Leviticus 23. The Sabbath was celebrated weekly on the seventh day, while six other feasts were celebrated yearly. The Lord commanded these feasts be celebrated so that his people would remember what he has done for them. Likewise, the early Christians saw fit to use the yearly calendar to remember important events in God's plan for salvation. These are referred to in the Church as liturgical seasons. You can always tell what liturgical season we're in by the color of the vestments worn by the priests and the colors used to adorn the sanctuary. They are as follows:

- **Green:** Used during Ordinary Time. Ordinary Time does not mean "boring" or "routine" it simply means the parts of the year that aren't connected to Christmas or Easter.

- **Purple or violet:** Used during Advent (The time before Christmas), and Lent (the time leading up to Easter). You may also see these colors at funeral masses along with black and white.
- **White and gold:** Typically used during Christmas and Easter.
- **Rose:** On the Third Sunday of Advent and the Fourth Sunday of Lent.
- **Red:** On the feasts of the Passion of Jesus and for the Holy Spirit. Also worn for the feasts of martyred saints.

(Triduum is a short liturgical season within (but not counted as part of) Lent. It means "The Three days" and starts the evening of Maundy Thursday and ends after the evening prayer on Easter.)

Depending on the type of church you came from, the liturgical calendar may have been something you celebrated. Many Protestants follow it. However, there are some who completely ignore it (usually with the exception of Easter and Christmas).

In my first year as a Catholic, I grew to love the liturgical calendar. When I was a United Methodist, we followed the liturgical calendar, but we didn't use the Lectionary (the prescribed readings and prayers). Every other type of church I attended didn't use the liturgical calendar at all. In your first year in the Church, you will have the opportunity to go on the collective journey through the plan of salvation with Christians all over the world by using the liturgical calendar. As you engage with it, you will experience some pretty amazing things. It's awesome!

Now that you are up to speed on your obligations, it's time to get to church. When looking for a new local church, you probably already have some connection. After all, you most likely went through, or are going through, RCIA (Rite of Christian Initiation of Adults) at a local parish. When you are received into the Church that will obviously happen somewhere. Perhaps that parish (Catholic word for "local church") will be your new spot. If it is, great; but if you find yourself needing to look elsewhere, here are some things you should be thinking about.

Welcome home!

As you meet Catholics who know you are a new convert, don't be surprised to hear "Welcome home" said to you. It feels good, but also a little strange because you are probably in a place you haven't spent much time in. It certainly doesn't feel like home, but it will. Home is a place you are familiar with, a place where you know people and people know you. These are aspects of what people normally mean when we say "welcome home." But Catholics mean something different. For Catholics, home is not about where you have been necessarily, but rather about where you really *belong*. Think about it. Even as a Protestant, you believed that ultimately this world was not your home. Your ultimate home is in Heaven. But how many of us have ever been to Heaven? Yet, we would all agree that Heaven is our truest home. Why? Because we know that Heaven is a place that God has prepared for us. Heaven is where we belong more than any other place. It's more "home" than anywhere (John 14:2–3).

For Catholics, the Church is an extension of Heaven on earth. Just as Jesus has prepared a place for us in Heaven after we die, he has also prepared a place for us before we die. That place, in a very real and literal sense, is the Church. It's where you and I *belong* more than anywhere else on this planet! Isn't that awesome? And get this—it doesn't matter where you are in the world. The Church is your universal home. You can be in another country, where you do not speak the same language or have the same culture, but when you enter a Catholic Church you belong. You are home.

This is a new paradigm for you. Chances are, the church you came from was understood to be your church home, but that had much more to do with your personal relationships and history there. It's not to say God didn't have you there for a reason, but it's a different sense of belonging when you really dig into it. I know it's hard to understand it all right now, but the longer you are a Catholic, the more you will feel it.

For some converts, that sense of home was something that drew us to the Catholic Church. The feeling was very real, yet hard to pin down. I used to feel a sense of something transcendent when I entered a Catholic Church. Even when I was nowhere near ready to convert, there was something that drew me into the physical places that just seemed like home to me. At the time, I would have attributed it to the architecture or art work, but now I see that there was something more happening. Being in the physical presence of Jesus in the Eucharist creates a pathway to Heaven that produces little pockets of home that even non-Catholics can feel. I bet you know what I mean.

What does all this have to do with where you go to Mass? Everything and nothing. You can go anywhere you want, and not go anywhere you don't want. Each parish will have its own set of rhythms, people, and culture, but in essence they are all the same in the sense of their spiritual heritage, doctrine, and core values. Styles will vary from place to place. Pastors will vary in their abilities, focus and personality, but they all fall under the same authority.

One key difference from where you came from is the competition between local churches over members. It is so prevalent in the Protestant (and especially in the Evangelical) churches; but it is no big deal in the Catholic Church. It's important to find a place you can get involved and put some roots down. However, don't expect there to be the sense of being courted by a local parish that is trying to convince you to join their parish instead of another parish. Those days are over for you. Your home church is bigger than that now. Home church is now anywhere there is a tabernacle containing the Real Presence of Jesus and a priest who has been given authority by his bishop to celebrate Mass. That's awesome. Different, but so very awesome.

What You Need to Do

Find a local parish you can call home.

This is where things may seem a little like when you were church shopping as a Protestant, but it's not the same thing. When you church shop in the Protestant world, you really have to be ready for anything. You can do a lot of research online, but a church website doesn't always give the most realistic picture of what you can expect practically. The experience you can have from church to church can vary so much that there is almost nothing that some churches have in common with others. I went to a church once that had a Dodge Viper on the stage because "it was cool." Other churches I've attended had a full liturgy that almost seemed Catholic. I've been to churches that require women to remain completely silent, cover their heads, and wear long skirts (pants were forbidden), and I've also been to churches that have women pastors (and even bishops) who looked like they just stepped out of a beauty parlor run by crazy people. Some Protestant churches are opposed to musical instruments of any kind, and still others have rock bands, sound systems, and light shows that rival the largest concert venues. In terms of theology, the variations are even more striking. You can find churches that teach that central to the Christian faith is the doctrine that the Earth was created less than six-thousand years ago in six (twenty-four-hour) days. Other churches will deny the necessity in the belief in the literal resurrection of Jesus. The list of important differences within what can be called a "church" in the Protestant world is endless. In the Catholic Church, it's not like that. There are some variations between parishes that are a big deal to some people, but the heart of it is the same. The doctrine is the same. The liturgy is (generally) the same, the authority is the same, and most important, the sacraments are the same. It's all home, and you're there. Now you just need to find your room.

Have realistic expectations.

I hate to break it to you, but there's no such thing as the perfect local church. Not even in Catholicism. I'm not talking about doctrine. I'm talking about humanity. It can be tough to face that as a convert, because you came looking for the "one, true, holy and apostolic church," and you found it! If you think that means that all individual parishes are perfect in every way, get ready for disappointment. There are some crappy

Catholic churches out there. Even though they have all the stuff that makes them Catholic, churches come with humans, and humans are the worst. They mess everything up. Even the most perfect institution on earth needs a supernatural promise from Jesus that the gates of hell will not prevail against it, in order for it to last (Matthew 16:18). It's not God's fault that his servants mess things up. It's God's grace that covers us even when we do. Therefore, since perfection is off the table, let's talk about what to look for as you begin your search.

Look for these things:

- A priest who teaches the faith and celebrates the Mass with complete reverence.
- A parish whose core value is faithfulness to Christ and is not trying to be popular with the secular world.
- A parish that has weekly holy hours of Eucharistic Adoration.
- A parish with people you enjoy and can see yourself spending time with.
- A parish that emphasizes the centrality of Jesus and the Gospel.
- A parish that cares more about faithfulness to the Gospel than what its members prefer.
- A parish with Bible studies, small groups and classes that are taught by qualified people who adhere to the faith.

Estelle's list includes:

- A church where the Rosary is prayed before Mass and the St. Michael the Archangel prayer is prayed after Mass.

This is a big list. You may not find a parish that encompasses all of these perfectly, but it gives you a place to start. You can decide what your priorities are, but realizing that finding the best local parish you can helps you more than anything in your first year.

How did I make this list? Where did these things come from? Simple. I looked at our local parish and started there. It's a great parish, not perfect, but great for us. As Estelle and I have traveled around and gone to other Catholic parishes, it has reinforced the idea about being home anywhere and everywhere. We often plan trips out of town around Mass times at churches. It feels amazing to walk into any church anywhere and know that we are home. That does not mean we have always had great experiences at every Mass we have attended. Our parish tends to be more traditional in terms of music and style. We like that. When we had gone to Masses where the music was, well, *different*, it hadn't always been awesome. That's just our preference.

"This feels like a cross between a really bad off-Broadway musical and a seventh grade choir concert," I once said to Estelle, as we endured a selection of "modern" songs that were inserted into the Mass. My rule of thumb lately has been, if the music was written in the 1970s or '80s and is played on a piano, it's probably going to have a bunch of people clapping during the songs on beats 1 and 3, and will be all about who "we" are.

I don't prefer the more contemporary feel, but it's OK if others do. I want the music in Mass to be about God. I want it written by a master who has been dead for at least a couple of hundred years, if not longer. I want the majesty and the power. That's why I converted. Don't get me wrong. I love contemporary worship music, just not in Mass, and certainly not sung by people as old as my grandparents. I'm sorry. I need to put my filter back on.

However, just because something is old and traditional doesn't make it awesome. I have cringed more than once at Mass when the song leader can't seem to decide which note to sing. I get it, not every parish can have world-class musicians at every Mass, but you have to decide for you how important that is. For us, it's a pretty big deal, but not nearly as important as the priest.

Finding a good priest is huge. I know that the Mass is about Jesus and the sacraments, but whether we want to admit it or not, finding a good priest can make or break your experience as a new Catholic. You don't need to find the next Billy Graham (a great evangelist) or Tim Keller, (an incredible teacher), but you need a priest who can preach and teach the word of God. I know that sounds like it would be an obvious requirement for a priest, but sadly it's not reality. I'm not talking about a priest being entertaining and fun to listen to. I'm talking about a man who can effectively and articulately preach the week's readings in a way that draws you into the mystery of faith. When you find a priest who understands his job as a preacher, you have found a treasure from Heaven. A good priest will make the readings come alive and help you understand why the Church chose to compile them for that week's Mass. A good preacher will point everything to the Gospel, and will also call his people to faith and obedience. A good preacher will have a sense of what his people need in order to be more faithful and encouraged in their faith. He will bring his best to the pulpit.

There's more to a priest than preaching. Priests offer the sacraments as they represent Christ on earth. You need to be looking for a man who takes that charge very seriously. You need to find a man who leads you to God and brings God to you. He doesn't need to be cool, hip, or even someone you would necessarily be friends with. Think of him more as a physician and less like a buddy.

This is different from the way you are probably used to thinking about your pastor. In many Protestant churches, the pastor needs to be hip and cool in order to relate to people and to reach them "right where they are" (meaningless church words for "anywhere they happen to be"). Or the pastor needs to be a brilliant communicator with an ability to take the congregation on an emotional and educational journey through the sermon. For Protestants, their church experience typically begins and ends with the pastor.

People in many Protestant churches want their pastor to be their idea of what they want to be as a Christian, husband, father, role model, etc. I remember seeing a "Pastor Wanted" posting for the largest evangelical church in a city where I had once served in a small church. One of the requirements was that the pastor must "be married with young children." The reason is because churches want not just the ideal man but the ideal *family* to lead them. I guess the apostle Paul, and even Jesus himself, wouldn't make the cut. You don't need your priest to be young, cool, or your buddy. You need him to be faithful to his charge, to teach the faith, administer the sacraments, and love and serve the people, as Christ has done. This new criteria may seem hard to live into because it's so different, but if you look for the right things, you will know when you find them.

Look for ways you can be involved with people.

Just like in Protestant churches, relationships are of vital importance to your faith. In your first year, finding meaningful relationships with other Catholics is of the utmost importance. So
where do you look? The answer may be surprising.

One thing you have probably noticed about the Catholic
Church is the lack of segmentation many Protestant churches
operate in. When I go to Mass, there are all ages, all types of
people, and all walks of life together worshipping Jesus. There
are no young adult, young married w/o kids, family, traditional,
spirited-traditional, blended, modern, country-western, youth
or children's worship services. There's just Mass. Everyone goes
whatever time suits them best. There isn't the idea that we all
need to be divided up according to our life stage or musical
preference when it comes to worship. Churches do that to try
to reach more people, but what ends up happening is a person
becomes trained to expect that the church will cater to their
every opinion and perceived need. Not to mention the silliness
when churches have multiple services, not because they need
the room, but because they have to keep people separate to
avoid a conflict. It's the spiritual equivalent to mom and dad
sending the kids to their own rooms during dinner. I lived in
that for so long. It was only when I started attending Mass that
I realized this wasn't the way it had to be.

Have you noticed it too? Have you noticed that when you
go to Mass, you aren't divided up into categories? There are
all types of people surrounding you, praying the same prayers,
singing the same songs, eating of the same body. Does that not
seem more like what the Scripture says? "There is one body
and one Spirit, just as you were called to the one hope that

belongs to your call, one Lord, one faith, one baptism, one God and Father of us all" (Ephesians 4:5).

This is one of my favorite things about being Catholic. So how do you find meaningful relationships? It's simple. Look around. There are people everywhere. They may not be the same age or in the same life stage as you are, but that's OK! What you have in common is more valuable than you can possibly imagine. Don't fall into the old pattern of thinking you can only be in a relationship with people just like you. That's not biblical and it's not Christian. Heaven will be nothing like that. So what can you do? Find out when people are meeting and go. Put yourself out there. Give it a try!

Each Tuesday morning at 6:00 a.m. our parish men's group has a chanted Mass, followed by coffee and discussion around a couple of tables in the church basement. The group of men that attend this group is pretty diverse. We have retired guys, newly married guys, young single guys, and many in between. There are corporate white-collar types, a guy who works second shift at a plant, and even some students. We all are very different. It's a great group. Our priest, Fr. Chris, invited me to it, so I started going. It was weird being the new guy, but I love being there. I love the relationships we share. These are not all guys I would probably hang out with, if not for church, and that's what makes it awesome! We are brought together by our brotherhood in Christ, and we all help each other grow in our faith.

There have been other opportunities for this kind of fellowship as well. A few weeks ago, I saw an announcement in our church bulletin about a group of people who gather together each weeknight in the home of a parishioner at 7:00 p.m. to pray the Rosary. I noticed that for a week they would be on my street. I knew no one, but I decided to go. I walked down the street to the address (I knew I was at the right house because there was a statue of Mary in the yard). When this nice little older woman answered the door and saw my scruffy face, she probably thought I had broken down outside her house or something. I told her I was there to pray. She smiled and welcomed me in graciously. There were five other people there, all of them much older than me. I'm guessing these weren't the kind of people I would ever be put into a small group with at any church. It was a great time. We shared a little about each other as a brief introduction and then we prayed together. There was no meal, no snacks, no crowd breaker or activity. There were no weird social expectations. We just came together to pray. A couple of days later, I went back and it was just me and the nice woman who hosted the group in her home. The two of us prayed the Rosary. There's no way in the world I would ever have seen anything like that in my former church life. There are good godly people all around you. Find some and spend time with them. Don't worry if they aren't just like you. It's better that way. You'll be glad you did.

What You Need to Not Do

Avoid the temptation to bounce around constantly.

A certain level of moving around may be necessary in the beginning, but the quicker you can find a home base, the better. It's OK to try a few different parishes, but once you find one you like, put some roots down. It's almost impossible to form relationships with people if you are inconsistent in attendance. People will know you by face long before they know you by name. If you don't consistently attend the same parish, people won't be as likely to find out who you are. It takes some time to become comfortable with the way things are liturgically, even in the Mass. There can be many variations between aspects of the liturgy, prayers, and worship between parishes. The goal is for these things to become second nature to you. That way you don't have to wonder which prayer is coming next, or how a parish might handle musical options. Remaining consistent allows you to focus more on Jesus and the sacraments and less on the form.

Do not compare your experiences as a visitor when you were a Protestant to what you will experience as a Catholic.

It's completely different, and if you don't understand why, it could be a little troubling. I'll go into more detail about the Mass later, but for now I want to focus on what it's like as a visitor and especially as a new convert.

Disclaimer: *I am fully aware that not all Catholic churches are the same, just as not all Protestant churches are the same. The experiences I have had shape my perspective, but yours may be completely different. There are exceptions to everything I am saying here. Take what is helpful and leave the rest behind.*

I have been a visitor in lots of churches. It can be a very awkward experience coming into a church service for the first time. When I was nineteen, I had just moved to Philadelphia from Iowa to play drums in a rock band. I was completely alone. Spiritually I was in a desert. I desperately needed to find some other Christians, so I began looking for a new church. Some Sunday mornings I would literally drive around looking for a church to try. Because I was raised a United Methodist, one morning when I saw the little sign on the side of the road that said "United Methodist Church, Turn right," I thought I should give it a try. I turned right!

What I found was a medium-size neighborhood church that had an unassuming look to it. I parked my truck and made my way to the front door. Like so many of the churches I had been in all my life, this one had what I call the Methodist Church Smell. Just like when you walk into somebody's house and it has a certain smell, I have found churches have that too. The bulletin boards with outdated announcements, and pictures of people at events eating food or working on a project, the large hanging felt banners lovingly made by a Sunday-school class, or someone's favorite aunt; the coffee, the people. It all felt familiar to me.

This church had two services, and I happened to arrive during the fellowship hour. I had some time to kill, so I just hung out in the narthex (fancy church word for "lobby") and looked at all the material on the Welcome Table. That's when Jack got me.

"Well, hello there, young man, I'm Jack!" he said enthusiastically. This guy was very friendly, which I appreciated. Jack was probably in his sixties and my guess was that he was one of the leaders of this church. He was still wearing his choir robe from the first service, which led me to believe that a traditional worship experience was coming up, which was fine. "Can I help you with anything?" he asked.

"Oh hi, I'm Keith. It's nice to meet you. I'm just here for church."

"Does your family come here, or something?" Jack asked.

"No, I'm new in town and just saw the sign for the church and thought I'd drop by," I said. Jack was looking more and more confused. Apparently nineteen-year-old kids in leather jackets and blue jeans didn't normally show up alone at this church just to attend a worship service.

Jack got closer to me, and his expression changed a bit. "Do you need some money or something?"

"Huh?" I responded.

"Is that why you are here?" He wasn't mean about it. I think if I had said yes, he probably would have given me some.

"No, I don't need anything like that. I just want to come to church." Jack nearly hit the floor. He couldn't believe it. He shook my hand and that was it.

About 8.2 seconds into the worship service, I had already decided that this wasn't the church for me. There was no one anywhere near my age, the music was not what I was into, and there certainly wasn't anything cool about this place. I wasn't going to leave before it was over, because I figured I'd at least stay to hear the sermon. In the meantime, I would just keep my head down and make for the back door as soon as the last song was into the last chorus. I was busy scouting the exits when we came to the most awkward time in the history of church services ever invented: *Welcoming Guests and Visitors.*

When you're not a guest or a visitor, this is a good thing because it helps you identify those people who you've never seen before. However, when *you* are the guest or visitor (depending on your personality), this is easily the most uncomfortable part of your day. When I was a kid, we did this in my church, but it was always voluntary. People would introduce their visiting family members, and once in a while someone would stand up and introduce themselves. There was no way I was going to do that. I knew I stuck out like a sore thumb already, and I didn't want any more attention. That's when Jack stood up from the choir loft, pointed right at me, and said, "I have a praise! Keith is here!" Of course, now everybody was looking at me and probably thinking, *Who the heck is Keith? Why is he here? Does his family go here? Maybe he wants money.*

What were they supposed to think? No worries. Jack gave them the lowdown. Right there in the middle of church. "Keith is nineteen and was just driving by and wanted to come to church here. He doesn't know anyone, but don't worry, he doesn't need any money."

What the heck was I supposed to do? It's not like I was running for president or something. I didn't want all this attention. I stood up, looked around at everyone, and said, "Thanks, Jack. Hello, everyone." People confusingly smiled at me. I sat down and thought, *I am not waiting for the last chorus of the last song. I am out of here during the pastor's closing prayer. When everyone has their eyes shut, I am GONE!!*

Because I was an idiot, I had written my new address on the yellow welcome card in the pew. I needed something to put into the passing offering plate, and if you don't have money, the yellow card is better than nothing. Although I told Jack I didn't need any money, I had less than five hundred dollars to my name and no job, so giving money to this church was out of the question. As planned, during the closing prayer, I bolted. I am sure Jack was crushed. He had probably made plans for how we would spend the day together before evening choir practice.

Needless to say my quest for a new church was far from over. I thought that particular experience was behind me, but to my surprise, two days later, guess who showed up at my front door? No, it wasn't Jack. It was the pastor! Apparently, the excitement of my visit caused quite a stir, and the pastor wanted to make sure I knew I was welcome, and that she hoped I would return. I invited her in and we had a nice chat. She was a very nice person and seemed genuinely interested in who I was and in finding out my story. I never went back, but I did appreciate her taking the time to come and visit.

In my continued search for a church I was never welcomed quite like that again, but more often than not, a visit to a new church and filling out a welcome card usually led to some sort of follow-up. This is because being welcoming and inviting to new people is typically a very important thing in most Protestant and Evangelical churches. That's not to say there aren't exceptions. There are plenty of grumpy, self-focused people in any type of church.

As a pastor, I spent many nights in meetings, attended seminars, read books and listened to highly paid consultants tell us how we as a church could be more welcoming and attractive to visitors. We knew that if we wanted the church to grow, we had to make sure that when someone new came into the church, they would be greeted at least seven times. We had clear signage that explained where everything was. We went to great lengths to ensure the church smelled clean and was brightly lit. We wanted smiling faces and warm personalities at all the entrances. We wanted to take away any awkwardness a person felt when they were new, so we ditched name tags and the Welcoming Guests and Visitors portion of the service. Because we understood that a newcomer would be unfamiliar with the rhythms and order of our service, we intentionally explained everything each week to the entire congregation as though they were all visitors. Anytime someone (even the pastor) approached the microphone to speak, we always introduced ourselves. Additionally, because our church had so many programs and activities, we wanted visitors to know about all of them. Multimedia slide and video presentations with professional looking graphics and nice music cycled on the large screens flanking the stage before the service. And of course, we had a world-class website, with professional photography and design. Whatever we needed to do to let people know who we were, what we were doing, and that we wanted them with us, we would do!

Does this sound anything like your local Catholic parish? I highly doubt it. I know there are exceptions, but when I started attending Mass, my first reaction was, *Does anybody even care that I'm here?* I know it sounds selfish, because it kind of is. In all my years as an Evangelical Protestant, I had come to expect that when a new person came into any church (even a Catholic one), the red carpet (that was brought over from Jerusalem in the fourth century, ha-ha) would be rolled out, and the new person would be welcomed enthusiastically.

This was not my experience. Many times I would go to Mass and there wouldn't be anyone greeting people as they arrived. At times there were, but they would just simply and quietly smile and hand me the missal. When I would find a place to sit, nobody came over to check on me or help me figure out what to do during the Mass. I either knew what was going on or I didn't. In my former church, if someone looked new, we trained our folks to sit by them and offer to help them feel welcome. This was not at all what I was experiencing as a prospective Catholic convert. I remember at Mass, even during the Passing of the Peace, reaching out my hand to the person closest to me, to have them shake their head and leave me hanging. What was that?!? I never once filled out a welcome card (never saw one), and I never had anyone from the church come to visit me without being asked.

I am not saying this to complain. I have been to many Catholic churches where people have been friendly. I am merely saying this because I want to help you, as a fellow convert, understand that the Catholic Church has a completely different understanding about going to Mass than what you are probably used to. If this catches you off guard, you may struggle a bit as you search for a church home.

The clearest way I can say it is this: in Catholicism *you* aren't the point. *You* aren't the focus. *You* aren't the priority. You being there isn't what anybody else is thinking about. Decisions are not made based on how you, or any other visitor, will feel or not feel. The Mass is not a service for you. It's an offering to God. I'm going to devote more time to what you need to know about the Mass in another chapter, but for now just understand this: Do not expect the Catholic Church to treat you like royalty just because you showed up.

Many of us have been spoiled by all the "guest services" we received as Protestants. I'm not saying there's anything wrong with Catholics wanting to be more welcoming and inviting. I know plenty of priests who would agree. I'm just saying that when you are first transitioning into going to Mass, and you're looking for a new home parish, you shouldn't expect the same type of "hospitality" you had in the Evangelical world. And that's OK. You will get over that.

Do not let your kids make the final decision.

If your kids are of the age where they will be coming to church with you, this can be tricky. Depending on the type of church you came from, your kids may really struggle with the Mass. Let's face it; the Mass is not designed to appeal to the instant gratification, highly digital, low-attention span, and excitement-craving desires of most kids. If you came from a church with programming and worship experiences specifically designed for kids, they may be in for a shock when you bring them to Mass.

My kids didn't know what to think the first few times Estelle and I brought them with us. We wanted so badly for them to love the Mass, but it quickly became apparent they weren't experiencing the reaction we had hoped for. They hated the music. They didn't know how to follow along with the liturgy, because even though the missal has the order of the Mass, there are so many options and variations, it's almost impossible to follow. Estelle and I were still learning, so we weren't much help. The kids liked the homily, but thought the chanted parts of the Eucharistic Liturgy were goofy. Even though we did our best to explain why they wouldn't be able to receive Communion, they felt excluded and hurt. "Why don't the Catholics think we're good enough? We love Jesus too," I heard several times. Despite the fact that in our old church, the Communion liturgy was subject to whatever the pastor felt like saying that particular day, one key point was always made. "Everyone is invited to receive Communion, no matter what." Obviously, as Catholics, we understand the biblical ramifications of this approach. But the openness and acceptance of all people when it comes to Communion, which is part of many

Protestant churches, is hard to leave behind for the children of converts. I've had plenty of discussions with my kids about the reasons why only Catholics in a state of grace should receive the Eucharist, but it doesn't seem to help them in terms of how they feel about it. At some point, our kids made the decision to stop coming to Mass with us. Their ages (twenty-one, nineteen, and eighteen) put them beyond the place where we could force them to come. The oldest two don't even live with us and our youngest is months from moving out himself. All of our kids love God and are active in their churches, and we are thankful for that. Maybe someday things will change, but for now, this separation is part of the cross we carry as convert parents of kids who are past the age where we make that decision for them.

What should you do when it comes to your kids? I can't answer that specifically, but what I want to help you understand is that the most important thing you can do for your kids is to be strong, joyful, and dedicated to your faith. Sometimes this means making decisions that your kids do not agree with or understand. It's great to consider how the kids feel when it comes to choosing a parish, but ultimately you have to make your choice based on what you think is best for your family in the long haul. Remember, it's your job as their parents to guide them and teach them their faith. If the Mass is hard for them to understand, make sure you are taking time at home to teach them. There are things you can do to help with this process. Have conversations about the faith. Explain things to them about why the Mass is the way it is. If your parish has programs and classes for kids/youth, take them. If they can find some friends there, that will help. Just like you had to learn and grow through things you didn't understand, so do they. It's doubtful your kids came to you one day and said,

"I've decided the Roman Catholic Church contains the fullness of the faith, and I want to receive Jesus' body and blood in the Eucharist. How do we become Catholic?" This conversion was your choice, not theirs. This is a big change for them. Have lots of grace, but don't let them call the shots.

Do not pick a church if the music or style distracts or creates a barrier to you.

One of the things that can catch new converts off guard is the variation between different Catholic parishes when it comes to musical style. Some parishes are very traditional, while others may be relatively contemporary. Depending on where you came from this may or may not be a big deal. When I say "contemporary," I don't mean to imply you will find a Mass with a full rock band like at some Protestant churches. You can find a parish with drums, guitar and piano, but I doubt you'll find too many with loud electronic dance music or heavy metal praise and worship bands.

For many people, the music used in worship is very important. In the Mass, music can be extremely helpful or horribly distracting. You need to choose a parish that has a style of music that helps you enter into the Mass with worship and devotion. If the parish you attend incorporates a musical style that makes you cringe each week, then it can be tough to focus. I'm not saying you should expect Grammy-level music at Mass, but if you find yourself constantly distracted, or put off by the music, you need to find a better fit. You may never find the type of music you experienced as a Protestant in the Mass, but that's OK. You may actually find something better! I love loud rock music. I was a praise and worship leader for years, and I understand the amazing power of good contemporary worship music. When I became a Catholic, I thought I would never quite enjoy worship the way I had before, when it comes to music. I've never been a huge fan of hymns. I love guitars, drums, and powerful vocals. For me, the thought of not experiencing the kind of music I love in worship was tough to accept, but I was willing to make the sacrifice. I also know that just having guitars and drums in church doesn't always help (there's nothing worse than bad contemporary worship music). I had resolved that I would simply have to learn to worship Jesus without loving the music anymore. Thankfully, something happened that changed everything for me.

One Sunday, we were unable to attend our normal Mass at 9:00 a.m., or our "we slept in" Mass at 10:30. Rather than look for another parish in town, we decided to try out the Latin Mass our parish celebrates at 7:00 a.m. The Latin Mass was never on my radar. I had enough trouble finding my way through the Novus Ordo (that means "New Order," but for most of us converts, it just means "regular" Mass). How would having Mass in another language be helpful? I wasn't very excited about it, but it was the right time of day for our schedule, and it counted, so the decision was made.

When we entered the church, things just felt different. I didn't quite know why, but I could sense something. We grabbed the regular missals along with the little red books that have the Latin on one side and the English on the other, and we took a seat. I noticed most of the women were wearing veils. There were always a few at the other Masses, but at the Latin Mass, that seemed to be more normal. We knelt and prayed. I asked God to help our family not appear awkward to everyone around us. I knew the Latin Mass was much more "active" when it came to standing, kneeling, and sitting. I also could tell that the people here were pretty hardcore Catholics. After all, you'd have to be to choose to go to Mass at 7:00 a.m. every week. I felt like we were going to stick out like sore thumbs. Lots of thoughts were going through my head . . . then the music started. Beautiful angelic voices from above and behind us filled the room. They sang in unison. I couldn't understand all the words, but recognized some of the Latin and Greek from my days in high school choir. What I did understand was that this was holy. Estelle and I looked at each other as if to say, "Are you kidding me? This is amazing!!" The entire service was like that. What we discovered that morning was some of the most ancient worship music in all of Christianity. It moved us in a way we hadn't yet experienced as new Catholics. We loved it immediately. I was also beginning to dig deeper into the chanted Mass before our Tuesday morning men's meeting. Through these experiences, I learned how powerful this type of worship is. I never would have expected that I would be a lover of Gregorian Chant (named after Pope Gregory I), but I am. When I am at Mass, I rarely find myself missing contemporary music anymore. There's just something "otherworldly" about this music. It's not about skill, style, or even melody as much as it is about a type of worship experience that comes directly from your soul. It reminds me of what St. Paul says about prayer in the letter to the Romans.

> *"Likewise the Spirit helps us in our weakness; for we do not know how to pray as we ought, but that very Spirit intercedes with sighs too deep for words."*
> *(Romans 8:26).*

Ultimately, the style of music is not the point. Whichever style of music you experience at Mass should be helpful to you. When that happens, few things can compare in this life. Do your best to find a parish where you can experience that.

Chapter 5

Who's in Charge?

Why does he dress like a Jedi? Why does he sing that way?

Once you've found your parish home, you're ready to dig into what it means to worship as a Catholic. There are many things you need to have on your radar that as a convert are going to blow your mind. Some are theological. Some are cultural and some are practical. Let's start with some practical aspects.

The structure of the Catholic Church is something that as a Protestant I thought made no sense. *Doesn't the Bible say the priesthood was done away with by Jesus? Aren't we living in the "priesthood of all believers?" Didn't Jesus say, "Call no man Father on earth, for you have one Father who is in Heaven?" Why in the world are priests required to be celibate? Don't the Catholics know that Peter and other apostles were married? How can a celibate priest help me as a father or husband when he knows nothing about it?*

What's the deal with the pope? Why should some old dude in Rome get to tell anyone else how to live? Isn't he just a political figurehead anyway? Find me the pope in the Bible! And what about all these ridiculous guys in their silly red hats? They all live in palaces. How are they anything like Jesus and his disciples? This is what happens when the Church becomes institutionalized.

These are all thoughts I had at one time. As I mentioned before, this book is not meant to be an apologetics manual. I simply want to share a little of how I came to see things differently, in the hopes that my experience may help you as you live into being Catholic. Often, things that seemed ridiculous to me were the result of my lack of understanding. Because I didn't care that much about learning the truth, I often didn't do any research into why the Catholics did what they did. Once I started on my journey toward Catholicism, and much more so even after I became Catholic, I learned the answers to these questions. One question proves to be THE ultimate question: *Who's in charge?*

The issue of authority is what led me, and countless others, into Catholicism. It's a dangerous question to ask "By what means has God provided for the faithful transmission of the Christian faith?" For Protestants the answer is simple: the Bible. After all, it is the "Word of God for the People of God," as we used to say after reading a passage in church. "Sola Scriptura" is the Latin phrase that means "by Scripture alone." This is one of the main ideas produced by the Protestant Reformation in the sixteenth century: that the supreme and ultimate authority for the transmission and teaching of the Christian faith is the Bible alone. In certain groups of Protestantism there are other things to consider (tradition, experience, and reason), but at the end of the day, the claim is that the Bible *alone* is what calls the shots. Everyone who converts to the Catholic faith out of Protestantism usually gets to a point where the idea of Sola Scriptura falls apart. It's ultimately a logically impossible position to maintain.

The concept of what makes certain writings "Scripture'' demands that God ordains an external authority. Scripture did not fall from the sky or magically appear in their accepted (even the Protestant) versions. The writings that comprise Scripture weren't officially declared Scripture until more than two hundred years after they were written. It's true that they were used in worship and understood to be authentic by the Christians right away, but so were other writings that do not appear in anyone's New Testament.

By what authority were the writings that comprise Scripture chosen or passed over? That's a tough question for those clinging to Sola Scriptura. To truly maintain that Scripture alone possesses the ultimate authority for Christians, it must be either believed that Scripture itself dictates to us which books belong (it doesn't), or that the Church simply ratified what everyone already knew. This is probably the most widely held position by Protestants. They know they can't produce a divinely inspired Table of Contents from within the texts themselves, and they cannot accept the Catholic position that the Church exercised her authority to declare the Canon (that would invalidate Sola Scriptura), so they have to say that somehow along the way, God just did some sort of miracle, and gave the Bible to the world, in spite of the Church. I have heard this doctrine called the "Preservation of the word". It simply means God did what he had to do to give the Bible to the world without the authority of (and in some cases in spite of) the Catholic Church. I used to think that way. That is until I realized two very important things:

1. The doctrine of Sola Scriptura isn't found anywhere in Scripture.

Sola Scriptura is blatantly contradicted by the Bible. Scott Hahn recalls in his conversion story the moment one of his students asked him, "Where is the doctrine of Sola Scriptura taught in the Scripture?" He had no good answer. It was the beginning of the end for Scott, and also for many others of us who had the courage to look a little deeper into the presuppositions we all make about the Bible and authority. I remember asking one of my seminary professors about Matthew 16:18. This is the famous text where at Caesarea Philippi, Jesus declares to Peter, "You are Peter and on this rock I will build my church..." The material that Devin had been giving me put forth the Catholic position that this was the moment where Jesus makes Peter the first pope and establishes his leadership over the Church. Honestly, I had never heard that before. The arguments seemed interesting, but pretty shaky. After all, how could it be that obvious? Were the Catholics really trying to prove the papacy and all its pomp and ridiculousness from Jesus giving Peter a new name? This had to be easily explained.

When I was in seminary, after class one day, I pulled my Old Testament professor (the New Testament guy was busy) aside and asked her about it. "The Catholics say Jesus is promising to build his Church on Peter, but what do we think about that?"

Her answer was simply this, "As Protestants, we believe Jesus is referring merely to Peter's *faith* and not to Peter personally."

"Well, why do we think that?" I responded.

"Because we're *Protestants*, of course!" Then she laughed.

Maybe a different professor would have had a better answer, but when I really began to ask these difficult questions, I came to the conclusion that for most of the history of Christianity, most Christians believed that Jesus did exactly what the Catholic Church says he did. That mattered to me. The answer "Because we're Protestant" was about the worst thing I could've been told. At the time, I was desperately seeking a way to convince Devin that he needed to leave Catholicism. All I needed to find was one doctrine that could be proven false; one time the Church changed an official decree of dogma; or one instance of a pope officially teaching a heresy. Surely this would be a slam dunk sooner or later. I needed to find a way to explain away all of these Catholic saints, doctors, and scholars who were explaining that Jesus did indeed institute his Church. I believed in the idea of the universal church, which was made up of all believers everywhere, but that was certainly not an institution governed by humans issuing decrees that must be believed. Or was it? Through reading the materials Devin gave me, I was exposed to the Church Fathers. Men like Ignatius of Antioch (AD 35–108), Polycarp of Smyrna (AD 69–156), and Justin Martyr (AD 100–165), and many others.

Who really were these guys? Why didn't I get the full story on them when I was in seminary? I read some of their writings, but what I realized was that I had been given a censored education about them. Most of the stuff that seemed "too Catholic" was either ignored altogether or explained away as the product of a different culture and time. So what did they actually say about authority and Scripture? Here are just a couple of examples:

> "[I]f you acknowledge the supreme authority of Scripture, you should recognize that authority which from the time of Christ Himself, through the ministry of His apostles, and through a regular succession of bishops in the seats of the apostles, has been preserved to our own day throughout the whole world, with a reputation known to all."
>
> St. Augustine of Hippo (Reply to Faustus the Manichaean, 33:9; NPNF 1, Vol. IV, 345)

> "See that ye all follow the bishop, even as Jesus Christ does the Father, and the presbytery as ye would the apostles; and reverence the deacons, as being the institution of God. Let no man do anything connected with the Church without the bishop. [...] Wherever the bishop shall appear, there let the multitude [of the people] also be; even as, wherever Jesus Christ is, there is the Catholic Church. [...] Whatsoever [the bishop] shall approve of, that is also pleasing to God, so that everything that is done may be secure and valid."
>
> St. Ignatius of Antioch (Letter to the Smyrnaeans, chapter 8)

Even the Bible itself acknowledges that there is an authority that exists in addition to Scripture. In 1 Timothy 3:15, St. Paul writes to his student Timothy: "If I am delayed, you may know how one ought to behave in the household of God, which is the church of the living God, the pillar and bulwark of the truth."

If you ask a hundred Protestants the question, "As a Christian, what do you consider to be the pillar and bulwark (foundation) of truth?" I would bet my last dollar at least ninety would say, "The Bible." I know I would have. But the Bible itself declares the *church* is the pillar and bulwark of truth. This was a radically new idea for me, but one I learned was more logical and consistent with history. Remember, the Bible came from God through the Church. If not for the authority of the Church, we wouldn't have an authoritative way to know what Scripture consisted of.

2. Without an authority beyond Scripture we have no way of knowing what the real Christian faith is.

The Bible is not functionally adequate to teach and guide the Church in and of itself. It must be explained. It must be taught. It must be interpreted. People may claim, "We just believe the Bible," but they don't operate that way. I have never been to a "Bible" church, where all they do is simply read the Bible. It's always explained, taught, and interpreted. If somebody wants to debate that, go for it, but I am not buying it. We all have our differences and own interpretations. How are we to know which is correct? When Protestants accuse Catholics of following man-made doctrines, they don't have a leg to stand on. Their own views on Sola Scriptura, and even salvation by faith alone (Sola Fide), were invented by men five hundred years ago. The truth is, we need the Church to teach us God's word, and to define for us what the nature and reality of the Christian faith is. That's the way God set it up. Read the gospels. You'll see it. You probably already did. That's why you're converting right :)? Me too!!

So what does this have to do locally with who's in charge? Everything! Your priest's job is to pastor his local parish according to his instructions from his bishop. The priest's authority is given to him by his bishop. Bishops are in charge of geographical areas called dioceses. The bishop is literally a successor of the original apostles. Apostolic succession is the idea that when the original Twelve Apostles died, the Church put a new person in place of the one who died. (Read Acts 1: 12–26 to see the first instance of this.) As new missions began, the apostles appointed others to serve and lead the Church. The pope is simply Peter's successor, and therefore continues in the ministry of "feeding my sheep" (John 21:15–17). Your bishop is one of those men who have taken on the actual ministry of the original apostles. His boss is the pope. The pope's boss is Jesus. That's the chain. That's what we participate in as Catholics.

Do you see why this is so awesome? Do you see that it's such an amazing thing to be part of a parish led by a man whose authority comes from Jesus himself? Outside the Catholic Church, anyone can declare him or herself to be a pastor, rent a storefront, grab a Bible, and start a church. It happens every day. You don't need to be ordained by anyone anymore. You don't need a formal education. You don't even need a license from a higher authority. You can do that yourself now. This doesn't mean that people who do this are necessarily bad pastors. In fact, one of my favorite Bible teachers to this day never went to seminary or became officially ordained. He just started a church in a meat shop and it exploded. Consequently, I know plenty of pastors who have master's degrees and were ordained by various denominations who can't preach to save their own lives. Here's my point: in Catholicism we have men who have been given their authority in a way that is traced back to Jesus—literally! In no way does this mean your priest is perfect. It doesn't even mean he's not awful. What it means is this: even the worst priest still brings you the best spiritual food. Here's an analogy that may help explain (but keep in mind, it's just an analogy, so don't follow it too far):

Imagine the Church is like a fine restaurant. The Church building is the dining room. The priest is the waiter. The bishop is the manager. The chef/owner is God the Father. The meal is Jesus himself. I know it's a little simplistic but follow me here.

When you go out to eat, you want the best service from a friendly, knowledgeable and competent waiter. It makes your experience very enjoyable, or very uncomfortable, but in the end your hunger is satisfied not by the waiter, but by the meal the waiter brings, which was prepared by the owner himself, who happens to be a master chef. Of course you want a good waiter, but would you rather have a great waiter who brings you an inadequate meal, or the best meal you've ever had served by a bad waiter?

Some might say, "I know where this is headed, but I would just go into the kitchen myself and get my meal directly from the chef. I don't need no stinking waiter." (It works better to say it in an Italian accent.) The problem is you aren't allowed back there. You don't work at this restaurant; you're a customer. You can't just march back and order from the chef directly, that's not how it works. You don't have the authority. Remember, it's his restaurant, not yours. *He* gets to decide how he serves his people their food.

Your priest is your waiter. He's there to serve you, but like in any fine restaurant, the waiter must be listened to and respected, because he represents the owner. You don't tell him what you want without first hearing what is being served. And in this restaurant, the food is the best there is, it never runs out, but there are no substitutions. This doesn't mean you control your waiter or are in any way his authority. This is a fine-dining experience, not fast food, where you "have it your way." He works hard to bring you his best, and you work hard to let him do his job. If he does a great job, that's excellent, but ultimately you came for the food, which he will certainly bring.

That's how it can be sometimes in Mass. Sometimes the priest is on fire. He preaches with passion. His words cut us to the heart and lead us directly to Jesus. He makes Scripture collide with our everyday lives and we are in awe of the power of God as he celebrates the Eucharist and leads us through the liturgy.

Other times, not so much. Once when we were traveling, we went to Mass at a parish we'd never been to before. We had our kids with us (which always causes Estelle and I to pray "Dear God, please let Mass be awesome today"), and although the readings that day were about the love God has for us, we got to hear a twenty-minute sermon about a documentary the priest had seen about the Beatles that week. It was awful. I felt so bad because we wanted our kids to have a great experience. They haven't followed us into the Catholic Church, so they couldn't receive the Eucharist. At least Estelle and I could endure this, and look forward to the sacrament, but for the kids this was unhelpful.

As you move through your first year in the Church, you will probably have similar experiences. Hopefully, you can find an amazing priest. He probably won't have the same degree of emphasis on preaching that your former Protestant pastor had, but that doesn't mean you won't have some amazing moments listening to him unpack the week's readings. When things are great, give thanks! When things are less than great, give thanks! You have something going on you never had before that isn't dependent on the talent and abilities of your pastor. You have the liturgy and the Eucharist!

Let's talk next about why he dresses like a Jedi. When I was a pastor, it used to drive me nuts when people would make comments to me about my appearance. Just because I stood in front of a group of people and preached the gospel didn't give people the right to weigh in on my clothes, hair, or face (all of which people did). I wasn't one of those guys who wore a robe. I thought it was pretentious and too "religious" looking. I wanted to come across as a regular person, someone who was down to earth. I chose to dress in street clothes because I didn't think my appearance was that important. I always prepared myself for comments whenever I wore a new shirt or anything different. The worst was when I would get a haircut. I knew I would have at least ten people (usually older ladies) come up to me and announce, "You got a haircut." Not "I like your haircut," or "Your hair looks nice," just "You got a haircut." Thanks, Captain Obvious.

Once, a woman came up to me right after I finished preaching and said, "I don't know how your wife lets you leave the house with your face like that." I think she meant to imply that I hadn't done a good enough job shaving. I shot back, "I don't know how your husband lets you leave the house with *your* face like that either." You should've seen the look on her face. It was awesome.

It's such a contrast to me now, but if I ever saw my priest without his collar, or saw him celebrate Mass without his robes and priestly vestments, I would feel scandalized. I know he's a real guy, but he's not *just* a real guy. He is someone who acts *in persona Christi* (in the place of Christ). He's a priest! In the Old Testament, priests acted on behalf of the people of God. They were a special people set apart for ministry and offering sacrifices. The role and duties of priests were dictated by God through Moses in the Law. Because of their importance in the plan of salvation and redemption, God prescribed in great detail how they would live, and even how they would dress (Exodus 28). Their garments and other clothing represented their unique and special status. A priest could not just show up to the Temple or synagogue in whatever he happened to be wearing that day. His entire being, even down to his clothing, was set apart and demonstrated who he was and the importance of his ministry. In Catholicism, so much of what we see and wonder about (because it's so different for us converts) has its roots in Judaism and ancient Hebrew worship, which centered on animal sacrifice. Because of Jesus, there is no longer the need for animal sacrifices or for a high priest who would perform them. Jesus has become our high priest and sacrificial victim at the same time. The book of Hebrews tells us that in some sense we are all priests (the priesthood of all believers) because we carry the message of the Gospel. However, just because we no longer need an earthly high priest does not negate our need for a new priesthood to offer sacrifice on our behalf. I know I'm getting a little theological here, but this has everything to do with why the priest dresses the way he does. Just hang with me.

The sacrifice of Christ on the Cross is the ultimate sacrifice. It was so powerful that it covered the sins of the world once for all, never to be repeated. This is a point many Protestants misunderstand about Catholicism, because they think the Mass is a re-sacrifice of Jesus. Not true at all. The Mass is a *re-presentation* of the sacrifice on Calvary that was offered once for all time. Not "representation" (it doesn't represent anything, it IS the same sacrifice), but rather a "RE-presentation." As in, the same sacrifice being made present again. For people who struggle with that, imagine it like this: Your mom makes the best Thanksgiving meal in the world. It takes her days to prepare it, and creates a huge mess in the kitchen. When the meal is served, it is spectacular and fulfills every part of the hunger you had before consuming it. The next day, your hunger reemerges and what do you do? You go to the refrigerator for leftovers. The leftovers are the same food you ate the day before, but did your mom have to go to all the work of making everything from scratch? Did she have to kill a new turkey or pig? Did she have to make everything again? No. She had done such an amazing job and there were leftovers. She could rest in the knowledge that her family was taken care of and they could continue to enjoy the fruit of all her labor for them. Now. . . imagine your mom is able to perform a miracle to make the leftovers never run out. That's where my analogy breaks down, but I think you get the idea. The sacrifice of the Mass is simply the miraculous leftovers of the body of Christ sacrificed on Calvary. It's not a new sacrifice. It's the original miraculously made present. Having said that (and this is VERY important) it's still a sacrifice. That's why there's an altar, and that's why there's a priest, and because he is a priest he wears his special garments demonstrating that he has a special ministry and is set apart for it. He's not just another guy. He has been given an incredible responsibility and an incredible honor. Now let me explain exactly what those garments are and what they mean.

The outer garment worn by the priest is called a chasuble, which means "little house." It will usually be decorated with a large cross on the back. The chasuble symbolizes the yoke of Christ. Underneath the chasuble, is the alb. The alb is a white linen tunic that covers the priest's entire body. It symbolizes the purity of Christ and the purity of the soul washed in his blood. Around his shoulders is a rectangular linen garment called an amice. The amice is placed for a moment on the priest's head. Then he places it on his shoulders and ties it with two long ribbons. This is to remind him of St. Paul's writings in Ephesians 6:17; *"Take the helmet of salvation, and the sword of the Spirit, which is the word of God."* Around his waist is a long cord made of linen called a cincture. The cincture symbolizes chastity. Around the neck of the priest is a four-inch wide band of silk that symbolizes immortality.

I know this all may seem a little over the top. Some of us converts occasionally saw our pastor in a robe, but others couldn't imagine their pastor wearing anything like this. I recently saw an article about how a younger generation of pastors like to dress in expensive high-fashion clothes, just like Hollywood celebrities, in order to be "culturally relevant." In Protestant churches, there is no standard for how a minister should dress. Like many other things related to worship, it's up to each church (or pastor) to decide. In Catholicism, everything has a deeper meaning. Everything symbolizes something.

Knowing the reasons why the priest dresses the way he does helps us to always be aware of what is happening in Mass. The Mass is not about the priest and how cool (or uncool) he is. His garments demonstrate that he does not belong to himself (or to the congregation), but rather to God and the ministry God has placed upon him. The priest is not trying to position himself in the culture by what he wears. He is showing that his role transcends culture by what he wears. Isn't that awesome?

Have you ever wondered why the priest sings or chants parts of the Mass? Why does he do that? The first time I heard a priest chant, I thought it was pretty funny. Now a beautifully chanted Mass is one of my most favorite things. Did you ever have that experience? Where did this practice come from and how will it contribute to your experience of the Mass?

The practice of singing (chanting) during worship dates back to ancient Jewish worship. In fact, the Psalms were sung during worship in the Temple. In the Bible we see examples of choirs of angels singing in worship of God (Revelation 5; Luke 2:13–14). Music and prayer have always gone together. The chanted liturgy of the Mass is simply an extension of that tradition. It may take some getting used to (especially if your priest doesn't have a great voice), but remember, the Mass is not a performance. The Mass is beautiful in and of itself, but sometimes the humans who participate in it may not have worldly talents the way we hope, but what is so great is that it really doesn't matter. What makes the Mass beautiful is not the talent of the priest, but the participation in the liturgy that brings God to the people and the people to God. Chanted liturgy in some ways makes it even less about the priest than if he were speaking. The chant equalizes everything. It takes away the pressure to say things a certain way, or to perform the way some preachers do when they speak. When the words are chanted, they transcend human communication and become something that draws our attention toward God.

If you struggle with this for a little while, that's OK. Stick with it and it will become beautiful. Worshipping God in a chanted Mass is an acquired taste. You have to train yourself to participate, but that's not a bad thing. "Worship" is about showing God's "worth". It's not supposed to be easy and without form. It should be something you have to work at. Once you do, it will make sense.

Now that you understand a little more about your priest, I want to encourage you to do all you can to appreciate him and his ministry to you. In the Protestant world, the pastor is, at times, treated pretty well financially. I know this varies greatly from church to church and situation to situation. I have served churches that paid me very well, and others who couldn't even afford for me to serve them full time. I know some pastors who are very poor (or also work secular jobs), and I know some pastors who are very wealthy. It's like anything else; the more "successful" you are, the higher your salary can become. The Catholic priesthood does not share this trait. There are no wealthy priests (at least, none who became wealthy by being a priest). There are very few, if any, external rewards for doing a good job as a priest. Priests work long hours with high, and at times, unattainable expectations from parishioners and others in their community. Many people assume that because a priest does not have a wife and children, he is available 24/7, and needs no time for himself. That couldn't be further from the truth. Even Jesus needed time for himself. So how do we take care of our priests? How do we show them that all of their sacrifice is appreciated? That depends on your priest and what speaks to him. There is no one-size-fits-all here. Some priests feel loved and appreciated when you invite them over for a meal. Others feel love and appreciated when you don't make them come over to your house. Some priests appreciate gifts, others would rather have an encouraging letter, or heart-felt thank-you card once in a while. But most importantly, if you want to show your priest some love, *do what he says.* Be obedient to his teaching and help him when he needs it at the church. When you ask for his advice and he gives it, take it. When he makes himself available for confession, go. When he asks for volunteers to help him accomplish something, volunteer. When you greet him after Mass, give him a hug and thank him for his ministry. In short, be a good Catholic, and even more, be a good person! Take care of your priest the way you would want someone to take care of your son, your father, or your brother if he had left everything behind to serve the Lord without the comforts of a family.

Chapter 6

Bells, Smells and Fifteen-Passenger Vans

Getting the most out of the Mass

Your first year in the church is going to be full of transition. Depending on what kind of church you came from, you will have some battles to fight. Those of you who come from more liturgical churches (Episcopal, certain types of Lutheran, etc.) will have an easier time adjusting than those of you that came from Pentecostal or more contemporary worship services. Another group of people who sometimes struggle with the transition are people who come from churches where long expositional sermons are the focus of the service. We will dig more into each group's potential struggles as we walk through the different sections of the Mass. I'm also going to point out some important things you absolutely need to know so you don't miss them.

Let's start at the beginning. Unlike where you used to go to church, it matters which door you come in. Catholic churches were built so that even their architecture makes a theological point. No one is going to stop you from coming in the side, and by all means, if there's a physical limitation that makes that the most accessible entrance, that's fine. But if you are able, enter through the front door. There's something about entering into the church and being struck by the majesty of the sanctuary. You come in at the farthest point from God, and as you move forward toward him, you see more.

I know not all the newer Catholic churches have this same design or feel. I went to a church once that made me feel like I was on the bridge of the Starship Enterprise. It was circular and white. The lines and decor were midcentury modern, and there were no statues. I had to look for a while before I saw the room off to the side where the tabernacle was. I know some Catholics hate churches designed like that. I know other Catholics love them. At the end of the day, it's not up to me to design buildings. I am not here to say one is better than the other, but my own personal preference is for the more traditional design. Maybe that's because I am a convert, and I don't want something that feels like where I came from. Either way, find the front door and use it if you can.

When you enter the church, you will find the holy water. Dip your finger in it and make the sign of the cross. This is to remind you of your baptism. At first it may seem weird, but soon you will instinctively look for it. Remembering your baptism may be impossible because many of you were baptized as an infant, therefore you can't remember it. That's fine. Remember that you are baptized. In Catholicism, baptism is a way bigger deal than in most Protestant churches. In fact, in Catholicism, baptism is the only sacrament that is required for a person to be considered a Christian. Baptism is the moment when a person is graced by God with salvation, and is granted entrance to the people of God. When you apply holy water to your forehead, you are reminding yourself to whom you belong. You are reminding yourself that despite all the stuff going on in life that can tear you down and make you doubt your faith, you are a child of God. Baptism happened to you. You didn't do it to yourself. You were most likely a passive participant. This is a powerful truth because even if you were old enough to choose to be baptized, you still needed someone else to perform it on you. This is a picture of God's grace. It covers us and comes to us, often without our even knowing it. It's the ultimate assurance that we belong to God. Doing something that reminds us of that as we enter into the church is a pretty awesome way to get things started. Isn't this Catholic stuff amazing?

Somewhere around this point you will either be handed a book, or you may just have to pick one up from a cart. The book is called a missal. It's kind of like the hymnals you mainliners (Methodist, Presbyterian, Lutheran) are used to. It contains the music and the readings for each day. You need this. Contemporary Worship People, don't skip this part. It's doubtful they will have the words to the songs on a big screen up front. Grab the book. One thing you may notice at this point that may differ from your experience is that it's probably eerily quiet. In many Protestant churches, the time before worship starts is noisy. It's a time when people are gathering and talking to each other. Kids may be running around, and sometimes the band is even warming up onstage. People are laughing and catching up on each other's lives, it's very social, and not usually a quiet place. I remember when I first started attending Mass, I felt like they must have just had a funeral before I got there. People were whispering if they had to communicate.

Some were on their knees praying, and it just had a very serious feeling. If I got there early enough, I noticed there was one woman off to the side praying a Rosary very loudly. I was tempted to tell her, "Keep it down, lady, you're not allowed to talk in here." I learned later that she was leading others in that prayer, not just having a loud moment to herself. If that's strange to you, try to understand that in Catholicism, much emphasis is placed on preparing to receive the Eucharist. St. Paul wrote that we must examine ourselves to see if we are in the faith (2 Corinthians 13:5). Also, that we should be careful not to receive the body and blood of our Lord unworthily (1 Corinthians 11:27). Sometimes, the time before Mass is just as important as the Mass. At my parish, there is always confession available thirty minutes before Mass, in case you need it. I would encourage you to start making a habit of arriving to Mass a little early. Not so you can talk to your friends, but so that you can prepare yourself for what is about to happen. Try it a few times. I bet you will see how different things feel to you.

If the quietness threw you off a bit, get ready, because it may change. Sometimes it's nearly impossible to hear what's going on once Mass starts because of screaming babies and little kids. I'm really going to ruffle some feathers here, but I'm speaking to converts who probably aren't used to all the noise caused by so many kids all the way through the Mass. You probably noticed all the fifteen-passenger vans in the church parking lot. That's because there's likely quite a few large families with lots of kids in your church. If you don't know why, go ask your priest.

Once, my son, Drew, asked me on the way home, "Dad, why hasn't anyone told the Catholics about having a nursery?" Drew had very little desire to participate in the Mass, but he was at least trying to understand the pastor's homily. This is a sore subject in lots of churches, both Protestant and Catholic. Some people think that kids belong in church no matter what, and others think it's too distracting for everyone else, and there should be some other place for kids who can't stay quiet. In my experience, more of the Protestant churches have taken the approach that there should be some safe place (outside of the sanctuary) for kids to be during the service. It may be a nursery, it may be a Sunday-school class, or a "kid's church" service with puppets and VeggieTales videos. Those things serve one ultimate purpose- getting the kids out of there, so the adults can hear the sermon.

Fewer Catholic churches think this way probably because the sermon isn't the center of the Mass in the same way that it is in a Protestant worship service. To be fair, I have seen Catholic churches that provide "cry" rooms, where parents can take their kids if they are having a tough time. They are kind of like a box seat at a stadium. They may even have a glass wall looking into the sanctuary and some comfortable seats. The idea is to make the parents feel like they are still there, while keeping the kids from being heard in the sanctuary.

So how should you handle this? Whatever you do, if someone's baby is having a meltdown during Mass, do not turn around and look at them! One of two things is going on: they are either doing their best to try to contain their child, and are very self-conscious about it, or they don't give a rip that their kid is bugging you. If you shoot a nasty look at the first type of parent, they will feel terrible and may decide next week to stay home (not good). If they are the second type of parent, they will shoot you back an even nastier look that makes you feel like a jerk for even being bothered by their precious little angel (also not good). It's just one of those things you will have to learn to manage. If it bugs you that much, try sitting as close to the front as you can. You will be able to hear better. If it gets really bad at certain Mass times, you may have to find another one to try. The thing you have to remember is that for Catholics, being at Mass together as a family is, in itself, a form of worship. The Catholic Church obviously encourages large families, so it would be hypocritical not to tolerate kids in church.

Estelle and I wrestled with this when we joined the Church. There were a few weeks when the screaming kids were so loud, and the parents were doing nothing, that I found myself literally becoming angry. We were trying so hard to learn and participate in the Mass, and it was beyond difficult. I couldn't understand why people didn't think about how their loud kids were affecting the people around them. Then something changed. Not *to* me, but *in* me.

Estelle and I had decided to start sitting as close to the front as possible with the older people (fewer kids seem to be there). As the Mass was beginning, a young family with little kids and a baby sat right behind us. *Right behind us!* I thought. *You've got to be kidding me!* Estelle squeezed my hand as if to say, *Take it easy, Keith.*

As the Mass began, it became obvious to me that mom and dad had plenty of talks with their little ones about remaining quiet. I could hear little whispers followed by gentle reminders from mommy and daddy to "stay quiet and listen." As the Mass progressed, the little ones became a little more restless. When the newborn would fuss, the dad got up and went out in the hall until the baby calmed down (this is why they sat near the front). Estelle and I could hear what the little ones were saying to their mommy in the way only little kids can speak, "Mommy, why is Jesus on the cross? I don't want anyone to hurt Jesus. I *love* Jesus, Mommy. When can *I* receive Jesus, Mommy? I *love* him."

Estelle and I looked at each other from the corner of our eyes. We knew we had just heard an incredible sermon, not from the pulpit, but literally "out of the mouths of babes." During the Passing of the Peace, we both turned around and high-fived the little kids and also told their parents, "Your family is amazing!"

That moment changed my heart. Don't get me wrong, I still prefer when parents take their kids out of the room when they are having a meltdown, but when I think about how many people use their kids as an excuse not to go to church, it makes me appreciate all of those parents who do what it takes to bring them. They don't need some selfish jerk (like me) to give them the stink-eye if their kid acts like . . . a kid.

Think about that. How long does it take you to get ready for Mass? How many kids do you have to get dressed? How many car seats have to be buckled in? How many diaper bags and bottles must be prepared? When families with lots of kids make it to Mass, we should applaud them, not run from them. So many in our culture make so many lame excuses for missing church. When parents with little kids teach them from their earliest memories that going to church is what families are *supposed* to do, that is a big win! We can all learn a thing or two from their example.

One of the things you have to wrap your mind around as a convert is that, in Catholicism, nobody is trying to make things easy for you when it comes to practicing your faith. If it's easy, great. If not, suck it up and do what you have to do. Sometimes going to Mass is going to be easy, with no distractions. Sometimes it's going to be tougher. There are crying kids, coughing people, bad acoustics, soft-spoken readers, grumpy neighbors, etc. You will encounter all of it and more. It's OK! We are all in this together. You'll get through it.

If you start to feel discouraged, remember, it's not *supposed* to be easy! Do you think the Hebrew people in the desert standing before God's presence in the Ark of the Covenant were complaining about screaming kids, or the color of the carpet (or sand)? Do you think the Jews in the Temple, gathered on the Day of Atonement, as the priests were offering sacrifices on their behalf, were rolling their eyes at that week's song selection? Do you think the multitudes listening to Jesus preach the Sermon on the Mount were fussing because there were no donuts and coffee left? In the book of Revelation, John sees a great multitude gathered before the throne of God for worship. Do you think they will have any concern for whether someone shook their hand or said hello to them?

What we experience at Mass, and who we experience it with, is all part of God's plan. We all have to remain focused on Him, and not ourselves. We have to see everyone else through God's eyes, not our own. When we do, we can see the treasure all around us, which are the people of God's flock. These are your brothers and sisters. In Mass, we are gathered at the family meal to worship our King. That's what it's about!

Let's keep going. As you prepare to take your place in the pew, it's appropriate to genuflect toward the tabernacle before sitting down. Just watch others to see how it's done. You have probably seen it hundreds of times. When I was first attending Mass (as a Protestant), I felt really strange not doing things like genuflecting. I felt like that stuff was for Catholics only. I wanted to participate and be respectful, but at some level I felt it would have been disrespectful to genuflect. That might seem very strange to some people, but I think most converts understand that tension. It makes sense when it's understood that the reason people (are supposed to) genuflect before the tabernacle is because it contains the physical, literal, presence of God. The Eucharist is the body of Christ. The more you come to understand that, the more so much of the "Catholic stuff" we used to not understand as Protestants makes sense.

When you enter the Church and prepare to sit down, genuflecting shows reverence for Jesus. In fact, whenever you pass in front of the tabernacle, you should genuflect to show Jesus that you recognize his presence. That's why, as a Protestant, I felt like I *shouldn't* genuflect. I had not yet come to a place where I recognized the Real Presence of Jesus in the Eucharist. What would genuflecting do? I had hoped I wasn't being judged by others. I just wasn't there yet, and I didn't want to pretend to be Catholic. Maybe you can relate. Maybe you never really thought about it that much. I invite you to think about it now. As a Catholic, the belief in the Real Presence of Jesus in the Eucharist is the center of your worship. Think about what it means that Jesus is truly present with us. You may be familiar with the last verse of Matthew's gospel, *"And remember I am with you always, to the end of the age" (Matthew 28:20).* As a Catholic, this promise means so much more than I ever thought. Jesus wasn't only speaking in a spiritual sense, but this promise alluded to his sacramental presence in the Church in the Eucharist. He's really here! He's really with us! When you consider what all that means, you will have no problem genuflecting.

The Mass may begin a number of ways. Sometimes, an altar server rings a bell and the priest comes out of a side room called the sacristy (this is where he prepares for Mass), and it starts. Other times, there will be a lay person who reads a brief welcome message (that will usually contain a gentle reminder to silence cell phones). Usually, they will say who the Mass is being offered for, and maybe a few other announcements. Offering Mass for someone is a way to help a person who has died. We remember them and ask the grace from that Mass to aid them in their purification before entering Heaven. Sometimes Masses are offered for the sick, or for some other intention.

Typically there is a procession in which the altar servers (usually youth/kids), the deacon, and the priest will walk from the back of the Church to the front. When I was a Protestant first attending Mass, one of my biggest misconceptions was that, for Catholics, the Bible wasn't really that important. After all, this was one of the standard lines I had heard from anti-Catholics all my life, among others, like these:

> *"The Catholic Church doesn't respect the Bible."*
> *"Catholics don't know their Bibles because the Church tries to keep it hidden from them."*
> *"The Catholic Mass is unbiblical."*

There are many other variations of this garbage, but when you are raised with only that perspective, you're bound to encounter some stuff in the Mass that will have you scratching your head. For me, it started with the procession. The altar servers usually carry a long pole with a crucifix on top. I had seen that before, so I wasn't too caught off guard, but it was what the deacon was doing that had me a little confused. The deacon was carrying, high above his head, a big red Bible. He carried it high, as if to show the people, "This is important! You all need to see this!" I thought that was awesome. It challenged my perspective that the Bible wasn't important to Catholics. Why would something unimportant be held high and placed with the utmost reverence right on the altar? What I have since learned is that when you convert to Catholicism, you are joining the most biblical Church there is. In fact, if it weren't for the Catholic Church, none of what you learned about your faith, in whatever church you came from, would have been possible. Anyone who pays attention during Mass can see that the ridiculous notion that Catholicism isn't biblical is just not true.

Biblical authority was a big deal for me as a Protestant. As my own denomination veered further and further away from the authority of Scripture, I had been so drawn to the reverence, emphasis, and obedience to the Bible that I had seen in Catholicism. It was one of the reasons I chose to convert. Many of my Protestant friends don't get that. They still think the Catholic Church is just a bunch of man-made traditions. They think that the Bible and Catholicism are at odds with each other, but they just haven't looked into it enough to see the truth. Maybe you can relate to that. Maybe you have people in your life who think you have left the biblical faith of whatever church you came from in order to join the unbiblical Church of Rome, which used to kill people like John Wycliffe for trying to get the Bible to the people. Try not to worry about what people who aren't Catholic believe about the Church. If they ever come with you to Mass, maybe their minds will change too! In the meantime, let's continue our journey.

> *"In the name of the Father, and of the Son, and of the Holy Spirit, Amen. The grace and peace of Christ be with you all".*

These are the first official words of the Mass. You can always count on that. As the priest says them, he makes a large sign of the cross. The people do the same.

> *"Brothers and Sisters, as we prepare to celebrate the sacred mysteries, let's take a moment to call to mind our sins."*

If you're following along in your missal, look on the inside cover for the Penitential Rite. It begins with the words "I confess."

Not every Mass has the Penitential Rite recited aloud. Sometimes there is simply a moment of silence where we are all supposed to acknowledge our sins. I love the Penitential Rite. I had seen variations of it before I converted in some liturgical Protestant churches (there are many things liturgical churches retained from Catholicism in the liturgy), but I hadn't experienced this in a modern non-liturgical church too many times. Recognizing our sin is a fundamental component of real Christian worship. If we come to Mass in pride and self-righteousness, we are way off the mark in terms of being ready to receive what God has for us. Jesus's story about two men who went into the temple to pray brings home this idea perfectly.

> [9]*He also told this parable to some who trusted in themselves that they were righteous and regarded others with contempt:* [10]*"Two men went up to the temple to pray, one a Pharisee and the other a*

tax collector. ¹¹The Pharisee, standing by himself, was praying thus, 'God, I thank you that I am not like other people: thieves, rogues, adulterers, or even like this tax collector. ¹²I fast twice a week; I give a tenth of all my income.' ¹³But the tax collector, standing far off, would not even look up to heaven, but was beating his breast and saying, 'God, be merciful to me, a sinner!' ¹⁴I tell you, this man went down to his home justified rather than the other; for all who exalt themselves will be humbled, but all who humble themselves will be exalted."

(Luke 18:9–14).

Have you ever wondered why during the lines "through my fault, through my fault, through my most grievous fault" we make a fist and strike our chest? It's so we can identify ourselves with the tax collector. Despite all the things we may do to practice our faith, when faced with the reality of the holiness of God, all we can do is beat our breast and cry out to God,

"Lord, have mercy, Christ, have mercy, Lord, have mercy".

Think about that. Cradle Catholics, converts, priests, deacons, bishops, everybody; we are united in crying out to God for that which we need so desperately—his mercy.

Sometimes the Greek words *"Kyrie eleison"* and *"Christe eleison"* are used. (No, they didn't get them from the Mr. Mister song from the 1980s. It was the other way around.)

Next, the priest, by his divine authority, blesses us and says,

*"May almighty God have mercy on us, forgive us our
sins, and bring us to everlasting life"*

Isn't being Catholic awesome?!?!?!

After the priest leads us in a prayer we sing (or speak) the
Gloria. This is a hymn that declares the truth about why we
are here—to worship God. The words are the most worshipful
stuff you can sing. It's deep and rich. One thing you'll notice if
you've converted from a church that uses contemporary praise
songs, is that the words of the liturgical hymns in the Mass are
completely centered on God and God's glory. Not all modern
praise songs have the same emphasis. Sometimes referred to as
"Jesus is my boyfriend" songs, some (not all) tend to stay away
from deep theological truths in favor of emotional or relational
responses to God. These are fine, but you'll notice things in the
Mass tend to be less about you, and more about God or directed
toward God. Again, I am not knocking all contemporary praise
songs. I still love many of them; it's just another example of
the type of thing you'll notice in your first year in the Church.
One more thing about the Gloria—not every church uses the
same melody. That can throw you off. If you don't know it,
do your best. If you go to the same church a few times, you'll
pick it up. One other thing to know—depending on the time of
year, you won't always sing the Gloria. A good rule to follow
as you learn is to let somebody else start. You don't want to
accidentally belt out a hearty "Gloriahhhhhhh" all by yourself.

Now you can sit down. If you're still learning when to sit and
stand, a good rule to follow is to watch the priest.

There are two main sections of the Mass, the Liturgy of the Word and the Liturgy of the Eucharist. In the early Church, the Liturgy of the Word was called the Mass of the Catechumens. A Catechumen was a person who had not yet been baptized, and therefore was not able to receive Holy Communion. This part of the Mass was mainly for instruction in Scripture and prayer. This is where the readings come in. In your missal, you can find all the Masses organized by date. Find the one for that date (if you are at Mass on Saturday night use the one for Sunday). Follow along with the readings there. These readings are called the lectionary. The lectionary is put together by the Church to guide the faithful on a journey of remembrance and celebration. The current lectionary was created in 1970 by a special commission charged with implementing the reforms made in the Second Vatican Council (look that up). The readings follow a three-year cycle. The cycles are referred to as Year A, Year B, and Year C. Typically there are readings from the Old Testament, Psalms, the New Testament, and the Gospel. During the Easter season (right after Easter), the Old Testament readings are substituted with a reading from the book of the Acts of the Apostles.

After the Old Testament reading (and the response, *Thanks be to God*), it's time for the Psalms reading (or singing). This is called an antiphon, and has been a part of worship as far back as when Jesus worshipped in the synagogue. Depending on how good your song leader is, this will either be something you really enjoy or something you wish was just read and not sung. As a convert, there is little frame of reference for what is about to happen. In your missal, you will see the Psalm for the day listed in sections. There is a line that is to be sung in the beginning by everyone, and then repeated after a few lines of the Psalm when just the song leader sings. Sometimes it feels like the song leader is cramming too many syllables into too few notes. Sometimes the notes seem random and arbitrary. It isn't really a melody, and it doesn't feel like a chant. I'm not sure musically what it is, to be honest, but I know the Psalms were often sung by the Israelites. This is probably why we do that in Mass. Either way, it's always awesome to hear and pray the Psalms.

After the Psalms comes a reading from the New Testament. Notice that the readings are usually a lot lengthier than what you are used to hearing read in your previous church. Unless you came from a Protestant church that follows the lectionary (some still do the same readings as the Catholics), you probably are used to the pastor taking a few verses and preaching a sermon in which those verses are used to make a particular point. Often, multiple verses will be used as proof texts to validate what the pastor is saying. He or she may use other texts to illustrate the point of the sermon, but the overall idea is that the Scripture readings serve the sermon. I know there are lots of variations here. Not all churches have the same views or practices when it comes to how much Scripture is read during the worship service, but my experience is that there are few church services outside the Catholic Church where more Scripture is read during the service.

After the New Testament reading, everyone stands and the song leader will lead everyone in a melody of "Alleluia." It will be sung once by the leader then once by the people. Notice what is happening with the priest at this point. He is preparing for the Gospel reading. If the deacon is going to read it, the priest will bless him. If the priest himself is to read it, he will say a blessing for himself. Next, a greeting from whomever will be reading the text, "The Lord be with you", and the response, "and with your spirit", precede "A reading from the Holy Gospel according to . . ."

Next, we all say "Glory to you, O Lord", and then we make a small sign of the cross on our foreheads, lips, and heart. This signifies that the Gospel affects our mind, our words, and our heart. Pretty amazing!

Next, the priest or deacon will read the Gospel. Standing during the Gospel is not something only Catholics do, but it certainly reveals the extra level of respect given to the words said by or directly about Jesus. After the reading is over the priest (or deacon) kisses the book and says "The Gospel of the Lord", and our response is "Praise to you, Lord Jesus Christ". After the Gospel reading, the priest or deacon will deliver his homily.

As I have said before, not all priests are of equal skill and technique when it comes to preaching. Hopefully, you have a priest who is able to explain and apply the readings for the day in a way that challenges and encourages you toward a deeper level of holiness. Depending on the type of church you came from, your experience with the homily may be very different. Things that may strike you as different may be the lack of themed sermon series that are very popular in many different types of Protestant churches. Sermons with catchy titles and culturally inspired themes are probably not something you will see much of in the Catholic Church. I have seen one church that turned a section of weekly readings into a sermon series called: "Giving: It's Not About You," complete with catchy graphics and yard signs near the parking lot. It's not necessarily bad or even non-Catholic to do that, it's just not very common.

When I was a pastor, I often felt a lot of pressure in certain situations to create clever sermon titles and other promotional material around sermons. I think it's because for most people who go to church, the sermon is the main point. People want the sermon to be deep (but not too deep), humorous (but not too funny), emotional (but not too sappy), challenging (but not too confrontational), and most of all the right length (I have been chewed out for preaching longer than thirty minutes and also for preaching less than twenty). The sermon is the main event and the preacher is the headlining act.

In one of my smaller churches, where I served as part-time senior pastor, one of my church members would persistently ask me every week for the next month's sermon titles. She wanted them for the newspaper. I felt bad for her, but I never gave my sermons a title. I told her this every week, but she insisted that people actually comb the Church section of the newspaper for interesting sermon titles so they can choose which church to attend that Sunday. She was not pleased with me when I said, "Call this week's sermon title: 'Matthew 4:1–17,' and next week's 'Matthew 4:18–25.'" She protested, "But that's not going to make anybody want to come here." I came up with what I thought was a great solution: I let her name the sermons.

I gave her the notes and told her to call it whatever she wanted. I have no idea if she ever did. I never saw the local paper.

Another church I served was filled with tons of creative people. We formed a group called the Creative Planning Team. Its job was to come up with creative ways to wrap our sermons in elements that were "creative." We were good at that. One Christmas season, we built an entire Whoville set from the movie, *The Grinch Who Stole Christmas*. Our sermon series was called "How Not to Be a Grinch This Christmas," or something like that. People loved it. In fact, years later, as that church was struggling with some tough times (many people had left for the new church in town with the cool people and the best band), someone even said to the new pastor (he told me himself), "We need to do some more stuff like the Whoville set to bring everybody back." He didn't agree (thankfully).

So why don't Catholics do more stuff like this? Is it because there are no creative people in Catholic parishes? Hardly. Is it because they never thought of it? I highly doubt it. The reason why is because, as important as the sermon is, it is not the main point of the Mass. Preaching is certainly an important part of the priest's job, but it's not the *most* important part of his job. And when he does preach, he doesn't need to get catchy and cute; he just needs to preach the readings. The Mass doesn't need hype or a gimmick. The Mass doesn't need promotional materials or slick advertising. The priest doesn't need to spend his time trying to be creative and slick. In reality, he just needs to get out of the way and let God's word impact his people. The Church has already given us the Scripture readings. Jesus Christ has promised to show up. The priest simply has to guide us into what is already there. He doesn't need to become the focus.

I once asked our priest, Fr. Chris, who happens to be a fantastic preacher, why he doesn't give a homily during the weekday daily Mass. He told me, "Because I don't want people to always need me to say something. I don't want to be the focus." I thought that spoke volumes.

Listen during the homily. Give your priest and the word he is bringing your utmost attention. You don't need it to be cute or cool; you just need it to be true. If you used to take notes during the sermon at your former church, you can still do that. If you like bringing your own Bible to follow along with the readings, then do it. There's nothing wrong with Catholics bringing their Bibles and notebooks to church.

What you'll discover as you continue to experience the Mass is that the readings and homilies have a flow to them. They aren't random and they don't follow the trends of the culture. They are usually related to the Church calendar, which is something I have found to be awesome. In Catholicism, it all flows together. The seasons, the readings and homilies, the music, and even the colors used to decorate the sanctuary, all work together to preach the word of God. The more you start to pay attention to even the smallest details; more things that once seemed disconnected will start to connect.

After the homily, the priest will usually (not always) sit down and take a couple moments to sit in silence. At first, for me, this was a little awkward. I was waiting for something to happen. I figured a musician or video guy in the back had fallen asleep and missed the cue to hit play or start the next song (transitions in worship services are always tough to get right). What was actually happening was the priest was letting us all have a moment to take in what was said.

Next comes the reciting of the Nicene Creed.

"Now let us rise and profess our faith".

The corporate reciting of the Nicene Creed was one of the things that God used to draw me into Catholicism. Some of the churches I worshipped in before did that, but I struggled to believe them. Let me explain.

As I mentioned before, most of my ministry was spent in the United Methodist Church. The UMC has an interesting stance on the ancient creeds of the Church. They recognize that they have played an important historic and theological role in the foundation of Christian doctrine, but the creeds themselves carry absolutely no formal authority. They are more like recipes from grandmother's cookbook than a rule book that must be adhered to. This hit me a few years ago when I was reading an article sent out by our denominational leadership called "Notes for Preachers." It was written by a retired UMC pastor who was pretty well known in our state.

The article mentioned that the National Atheist Convention had recently been held in Des Moines. He said one thing that struck him was that he felt we, as United Methodists, had more in common with the atheists than with the "fundamentalists," because "at least we weren't running around telling everyone they were going to hell." I had grown accustomed to much of the (in my opinion) ridiculous unbiblical stuff in articles like this, but for some reason I decided I needed to write this guy. I sent him an email asking him how he thought it was possible for atheists, who denied the existence of God and every single line of even the most fundamental creeds of Christianity, to have more in common with us than a fundamentalist, who despite certain theological differences, could with good conscious adhere to the creeds. His response to me was this: "If you had gone to a United Methodist seminary (I never told him where I went), you would know that we United Methodists are not bound to the creeds, as we are not a Creedal Church." This means that there was no creed that universally defined what United Methodists believed. I was a little shocked to hear this, but after doing a little digging, I learned that he was indeed correct. Over the course of the years, as I saw more and more division and departure from what I considered to be orthodox and basic Christian doctrine, I recognized that the lack of a clear objective definition of what the Christian faith was and taught led to all sorts of chaos.

I knew that there were lots of different interpretations of Scripture and what were considered to be nonessentials in the various Protestant churches, but I thought at the very least we could all agree on the Nicene Creed as authoritative. What I learned was the ancient creeds may or may not carry much weight in various Protestant churches. They can say them in worship services once in a while, but if they don't view them as authoritative, then it's nothing more than lip service, or, dare I say "vain repetitions."

When I started attending Mass, even as a Protestant, I found myself refreshed and strengthened standing with other Christians and professing our faith aloud, together, for real. Knowing that this Church had unwaveringly held to and declared the truths of the Creed pulled me into a place of safety and assurance that even when human beings fail and fall away, the Creed remains. The Creed declares to us, and to the whole world, that despite all the compromise and capitulation of many modern Protestant churches, there are certain doctrinal truths that define what the Christian faith is. Churches can have their "Statements of Faith" and all of that, but at the core, the Nicene Creed declares the central truths of the Christian Faith. When we stand together and profess it, we are grounded, unified and accountable. This is what makes us Christians—believing and living out the truths contained in this creed. So when it's time to stand and profess, do it boldly, from the heart, with humility and pride at the same time. Humility in that you submit yourself to it, pride in that you would die for it. For many have.

After the Creed is recited, the Prayer of the Faithful is offered to God. This is done usually by a reader standing at the pulpit. The person reads the prayer, and then the faithful respond out loud, *"Lord, hear our prayer"*. Sometimes these prayers may seem a little generic ("we pray for everyone in the world who is sick and suffering, etc".), but they will also become very specific to the needs of the parish and community. There is normally a short space made for our own specific intentions. "Intentions" is Catholic for "requests." Maybe you grew up in a church that used the word "intentions," but for me it was always prayer "requests." It's the same thing.

During the prayers, I like to imagine that all of the things in my heart I am asking God are being united with all the prayers of the people gathered. And not only those gathered, but all the Saints together. If you attend a Mass that uses incense, imagine your prayers being carried to God with the smoke of the incense (Revelation 8:4). We bring all of these intentions to God together, asking with worshipful hearts, *"Lord, hear our prayer."* Not just my prayer, but *our* prayer. We are a family, and we come to God together.

After the prayer, everyone is seated and the offering begins. As far as church offerings go, I would say that most offering times in Catholic churches are pretty laid back. Lots of churches have different philosophies and methods of collecting the weekly offering. I have seen many. At one Pentecostal church I attended, everyone was ushered out of their seats and brought to the front of the stage where the pastor stood holding a giant bucket. Every person had to pass by the pastor and either put something in or not. He would stand there literally looking at each person. Can you imagine what that must feel like if you don't put something in? I remember one Sunday he even said, "Everybody should put something in. If you didn't bring anything for God, turn to your neighbor and borrow something from him." I am not making this up. Other churches, in a desire to be less pushy, have skipped this portion of the service altogether. Instead of passing a plate or basket, they will have a box in the back and people can discreetly place their gifts there without feeling pressure or the awkwardness that comes from passing a plate by without putting anything in.

Have you ever thought of the offering time as holy? If not, I understand. Perhaps it's because it is rarely treated as such in most churches. There's almost always something else unrelated to the offering going on. It's either an announcement, a "ministry highlight"—aka infomercial—performance song, or video, etc. In many churches, the offering is treated as a transition time (usually between the music and the sermon).

When I was a pastor, the offering time was always a mixed bag, because we weren't sure what else should be happening during that time. To be honest, I never really gave that part of the service much thought until something happened at my last church. A man expressed to our senior pastor, "Don't mess with the offering time. For me, it's the most important time of the service. I come to hear a message and give my gifts to God. Don't clutter it with announcements." I had never thought of it that way before, but it made a lot of sense to me. When we became Catholic, for the first time in my adult life I actually sat in the pews during the offering. I said to Estelle, "This is a big moment in the worship service." She recognized that I felt that way, and now gives me the gift to put into the basket as it makes its way through the pews. For me, it's become a big deal. We don't have a lot of money, but we feel honored to give to the Lord's work in his Church.

I'm not saying that in the Mass, angel feathers fall from the sky when the baskets are passed. But I do think it's interesting and worth mentioning that while the offering is being taken, nothing more happens other than the singing of a hymn, while the priest makes preparations for the Eucharist. As the offering time ends, a lay person (or a family) brings the bread and wine to the priest, along with the gifts of the people. It's as if all of what is brought forth in our offerings is to be joined with what will now be offered to God for us, the body and blood of Christ.

This is the natural break between the Mass of the Catechumens and the Mass of the Faithful. In the ancient Church, this was the moment when the non-baptized people would leave.

This portion of the Mass is what distinguishes Catholics from virtually every other form of Christianity on the planet.

It's likely that for many of you, the Liturgy of the Eucharist isn't something you have never seen before; it's just that in Catholicism, what happens on the altar isn't simply a memorial meal or celebration of a symbol. For Catholics, the celebration of the Eucharist is a fulfillment of the Jewish Passover feast. In short, this means that the Mass is actually a sacrifice.

The Passover was one of the seven feasts that God commanded the Hebrews to celebrate after their escape from Egypt. You can read about the original Passover in Exodus 12. The basic idea is that the Israelites were slaves in Egypt for hundreds of years. Moses was called by God to declare to the Pharaoh, "Let my people go." If you've seen *The Prince of Egypt, The Ten Commandments*, or listened to the Metallica song "*Creeping Death*," you know the story. Pharaoh refuses. God sends plagues and bad things happen. Pharaoh still will not relent, so God moves through Egypt and strikes dead all the firstborn sons. The only households spared were those who, by Moses' instruction, applied the blood of a slaughtered lamb to their doorpost. One important aspect of this event was that the Hebrews were commanded to eat this lamb. *"The blood shall be a sign for you on the houses where you live: when I see the blood, I will pass over you, and no plague shall destroy you when I strike the land of Egypt." (Exodus 12:13).* This meal has become the basis for the Jewish Passover feast, which has been fulfilled in the Last Supper.

The following day Pharaoh was overcome with grief at the death of his son and all the others. He then released the slaves from the land. He quickly changed his mind and pursued the Israelites, until ultimately perishing with his armies in the

Red Sea, after Moses led the Israelites safely through, by the miracle of God parting the waters.

This event led to the freedom from slavery, and ultimately to the entrance of the Israelites into the Promised Land. The people of God were commanded to celebrate this feast, as it pointed both backward to the way God delivered them, and forward to the coming of Jesus, who would become the ultimate Passover lamb. Jesus' sacrifice on Calvary would serve as the gateway for God's people to be freed not from worldly slavery, but even more importantly from the slavery of sin and death. His body and blood were offered up for all the world, once for all. Therefore, when the blood of the lamb is applied to the soul of a person, death passes over them, and they are given entrance into the eternal Promised Land, Heaven. There is so much to be said about the relationship between the sacrifice of the Mass and the Passover.

This relationship was foreshadowed by John the Baptist, when he proclaimed Jesus as *"the lamb of God who takes away the sin of the world" (John 1:29)*. Additionally, St. Paul wrote to the Corinthians: *"Clean out the old yeast, so that you may be a new batch, as you really are unleavened. For our paschal lamb, Christ, has been sacrificed." (1 Corinthians 5:7)*.

Jesus himself made the connection complete when at his Last Supper (which was a Passover meal) he instituted the Eucharist, forever revealing himself to be the ultimate Passover lamb. The Eucharistic Liturgy is in essence the fulfillment of the command Jesus gave to his disciples at the Last Supper to "do this in memory of me". Every time a priest offers Mass, he is doing exactly what Jesus commanded.

The liturgy walks us through that very act, but unlike most Protestant Communion services, the Mass is understood not simply as a memorial meal, but as a sacrifice. But not just any sacrifice: the Mass is a participation in the sacrifice of Jesus on Calvary. It's not an additional sacrifice, it is the same sacrifice miraculously made present. This is a nuanced but profoundly important point.

Volumes have been written about this. I don't intend to cover it all here, but suffice it to say, the sacrificial nature of the Mass and the Real Presence of Jesus in the Eucharist is the key to understanding why so much of the Mass is the way it is. (Remember, this is why we genuflect before the tabernacle). As the priest begins his sacred duty of leading his people through the Liturgy of the Eucharist, he prays for God to cleanse him of his own sin. Unlike Jesus, the priest understands that he is in need of the forgiveness that comes through the sacrifice of Jesus. He stands at the middle of the altar and faces the people and says,

> *"Pray brethren, that my sacrifice and yours may be acceptable to God, the almighty Father".*

The people respond,

> *"May the Lord accept the sacrifice at your hands, for the praise and glory of his name, for our good, and the good of all his Holy Church".*

As we all journey through the liturgy together, you need to understand that the responses you make are key. In the Mass, the people aren't simply there to watch. We participate with our words and with our bodies. All of the standing, sitting, kneeling, singing . . . it's all designed to bring us to this place of worship that joins Heaven and earth.

If you've ever seen art in Catholic books depicting the Mass being offered with angels and saints above the altar participating alongside the faithful, you can get a sense of what is truly happening. The Mass is literally a joining together of Heaven and earth.

That's what we are doing. We are participating in the once and for all sacrifice on Calvary that John sees in the book of Revelation, and that we see in Isaiah's vision in chapter 6. Next, we sing,

> *"Holy, Holy, Holy Lord God of hosts. Heaven and earth are full of your glory. Hosanna in the highest, blessed is he who comes in the name of the Lord, Hosanna in the highest."*

The latter part of this hymn comes from the greeting that Jesus was given as he entered into Jerusalem on Palm Sunday. His purpose for entering the city was to offer himself as the sacrifice for our sins. Much in the same way as we participate in the sacrifice of the Mass, we welcome him into the Church and into our hearts. That's why immediately following this hymn we kneel.

Does it seem strange to you to have all this kneeling as part of your worship? I remember when I first started attending Mass, it seemed weird to me. Lots of things did. Anything that seemed too programmed or ritualistic made me think of people just going through the motions of some religious duty. It made me think of Jesus' harsh words about "vain repetitions" and "doctrines of man." I saw all of the liturgical prayers and formulas as lifeless and stale. All I could think of was the way Jesus came to free the Jews from all of their religious traditions and usher in this new faith that was personal and free-flowing. Catholicism (and other liturgical forms of worship) seemed to me to embody the opposite of what Jesus came to do. "I'm a Christian, but not religious," was the kind of thing many Evangelical Protestants said, and I affirmed that idea. The idea of being religious was almost an insult. If you aren't used to a liturgical worship experience, the Liturgy of the Eucharist may be strange at first, but I promise it will become more meaningful than you can ever imagine.

The words spoken (and sung) in the liturgy, *"Take this all of you and eat of it, for this is my body which will be given up for you. Do this in memory of me"*, are the exact words Jesus used at the Last Supper. Isn't it strange when Protestants object that Catholics aren't biblical? These words are required for a Mass to be valid. No priest can decide to change them or paraphrase them. They must be used exactly in this way.

Can you think of many Protestant churches where a biblical liturgy like this is mandated? In most churches, a pastor can say any number of things during the Communion liturgy. When I was wrestling with converting to Catholicism, the most difficult to hear was when our senior pastor would say,

> *"Jesus took bread, broke it, gave it to his disciples and said, 'This bread represents my body, as long as you eat this bread remember that you are the body of Christ.'"*

Even when I was still a Protestant, I had a hard time with this. Jesus never said "represents," he said this "is." For crying out loud, even Martin Luther insisted on that point. Make no mistake about it. The Mass is more biblical than anything else going on in this world.

Our priest often chants the words of the liturgy. At first I didn't know if I could get used to it, but after some time, I find myself singing those words during the day. The chanting is not about trying to sound holy or something. It's meant to be a beautiful way to pray. Prayer and music have always gone together. The beautifully chanted liturgy is a treasure. Let the liturgy guide you into the throne room of God. This is what it's intended to do, and when added to a faithful heart, that's exactly what will happen.

During this portion of the Mass, everyone will stand and will pray the Our Father. We always called it the Lord's Prayer in all the churches I attended. I'm not sure if there is any particular reason why. Much of this will seem the same as when you prayed the prayer as a Protestant, but there is one key difference. In the Mass, the Our Father ends after the words, *"but deliver us from evil"*. The first few times I attended Mass I thought, *These Catholics skipped the ending.* It took me a little while to realize that the end of the prayer is actually the way the Catholics pray it. See Matthew 6:13. I was so used to ending the prayer with, "For thine is the kingdom, and the power, and the glory, forever. Amen," I guess it never really hit me that what I thought was part of Jesus' actual prayer was a variation of the Roman Catholic response to the prayer in the Mass, which many Protestants just rolled right into the prayer itself. I know those extra words were part of the King James translation, but it's rare to find another translation that includes them.

The priest continues by saying:

> *"Deliver us, Lord, we pray from every evil, graciously grant peace in our days, that, by the help of your mercy, we may be always free from sin and safe from all distress, as we await the blessed hope and the coming of our Savior, Jesus Christ.*

This is when we say,

> *"For the kingdom, the power and the glory are yours, now and forever."*

Sometimes you may go to a Mass where this entire prayer is sung. For me, that is one of the most special parts of the Mass. I love hearing everyone sing the prayer together. For some reason the voices singing in unison gives me chills. At first, singing the prayers seems strange, but stick with it. Soon you will find yourself singing these prayers while driving down the road or taking a shower. I bet God loves that!

Have you ever noticed that during the Our Father some people raise their hands, and some hold hands with those around them? Others don't, and may even refuse if you reach for their hand. What's happening here is a bit of a liturgical family feud. The Orans (Latin for "praying") posture is the technical term for what the priest is doing. It's his job as the priest to represent God to his people and represent his people to God. This is what that posture means. Although in many parishes it seems as if everybody does this, it's technically not part of the rubric (rules) of the Mass. I once asked a priest about this and he said it's not correct for laypeople to do that, but most priests don't want to make a huge deal out of it so they say nothing. Can you imagine a priest stopping the liturgy to scold the people? "Put those hands down! That's my job"!

I know some more traditional Catholics would applaud and cheer (after Mass, of course), but that's a battle for another time. As for me and my wife, our policy has been not to raise or hold our hands during the Our Father, but if some sweet little old lady grabs my hand, I'm not going to leave her hanging. It's not as if people who raise their hands during the prayer are committing a heinous sin. It makes them feel like they are participating more fully. I'm not going to do it, but it's not my job to police them. If it's that big a deal, the priest should say something.

After the Our Father, another interesting time for converts is the Sign of Peace (this is the Catholic version of The Passing of the Peace- it's basically the same thing). This is one of those things that you'll learn that some Catholics love and others barely tolerate. I always get a kick out of watching people during this time. There are those who keep their passing confined to people immediately near to them. There are others who try to make it around as much of the church as possible, but due to time constraints are forced to smile and wave around the room (I call it the "parade wave"). There are also those who either have no peace to pass or too much peace to take some of mine. More than once, I have turned around in a pew to pass some peace, only to have my peace blocked by a nasty look, a shaking of the head, or a refusal to even acknowledge it. Estelle and I have talked about that situation many times. What do we do? Here's what I have come up with.

I start by hugging my wife, and maybe even a small kiss on the cheek. Then, I make a counterclockwise circle and extend a hand to whoever is close enough to shake. *"Peace be with you,"* is the expected and sufficient greeting, so we stick with that. If somebody waves me off, I keep the circle going until I'm back to where I started. If I happened to notice someone I know personally in church, I will try to do the "parade wave" at them so there's at least some acknowledgment there. That's usually all there is time for.

This whole thing is a little different than the "turn and greet those around you" time in the services many Protestants are used to. In my last church, those times usually lasted much longer and people were often a little more mobile and conversational.

What's interesting to us are the times we've attended a more contemporary Catholic parish that does both. Before the Mass officially begins, there's the "turn and greet those around you" time. Then, during the liturgy, we get to do it all over again with the Passing of the Peace. That seems a little awkward, but whatever. Here's what I am usually thinking: *Do I pass the peace to the same people I greeted earlier, or does that make me seem too needy? What if I miss someone close to me both times? They will think I hate them. Wait, why did that guy not greet or pass me his peace? What a jerk!*

Sometimes, trying to insert too much social interaction can make things awkward. I'm sure other people think it's the best part of the day. Just do your best. Smile at people and be nice. It will all be fine.

After the peace has been passed, we have come to the center of the entire Mass. This is the moment when we worship Jesus in the Eucharist and declare who he is (*"Lamb of God"*) and what he does (*"you take away the sins of the world"*), and ask that his grace be applied to our hearts (*"have mercy on us"*). Sometimes even in vernacular Masses this next part is said or sung in Latin: *"Agnus Dei . . ."* This is repeated three times, but the last time, the words "grant us peace" replace "Have mercy on us." Then we kneel.

> *"Behold, the Lamb of God, behold Him who takes away the sins of the world. Blessed are those called to the supper of the Lamb."*

These are the words spoken by the priest as he holds up the consecrated host and the chalice. These are the most important words anyone will say to you all week. You need to understand that, as a Catholic, you believe this is literally true.

"Behold, the Lamb of God" is a direct quote from the words of John the Baptist in John 1:29. John said this to his disciples as he saw Jesus walking. John the Baptist was the forerunner of Jesus. It was his job to get people ready to encounter Jesus. He baptized people and told them that one was coming *"whose sandals I am not worthy to untie" (John 1:27). "He will baptize you with the Holy Spirit and fire" (Matthew 3:11).*

John's father was a priest named Zechariah. It is certain that John was raised with a deep knowledge of all things Jewish. Scripture, prophecy, and religious life were all things John the Baptist knew well. It is John who first connects Jesus with the prophecies of Isaiah 53, and the imagery of the Passover lamb.

It's as if John knew not only who Jesus truly was, but also what his divine purpose was.

This declaration of the identity and mission of Jesus is the center of the Gospel. Jesus is not just another religious teacher with some great tips on how to live a moral life. Jesus is God and man at the same time. Jesus offers himself up for us as our Passover lamb so that we can be freed from the penalty of sin and have eternal life. I know many Protestants don't think Catholicism teaches this, but they are just plain wrong. Catholicism declares the gospel in every Mass.

When we kneel as the priest recites these words, *"Behold the Lamb of God,"* understand this is a command to us. We are being told to do exactly that. Behold him! Don't miss this. It will change everything about the way you worship Jesus. I am often emotionally moved to the point of tears during this part of the Mass. Everything we have done and said up to this point has led us now to the moment when our priest consumes the body of Christ and then prepares to offer it to us. The people then say together, *"Lord I am not worthy that you should enter under my roof, but only say the word and my soul shall be healed."*

This response is taken from the words of the Roman centurion who encountered Jesus and asked him to heal his servant (Matthew 8:5–13). Jesus told him he would travel to the man's home to heal him. The centurion's response was, *"Lord, I am not worthy to have you come under my roof, but only speak the word and my servant will be healed."* Jesus responded by saying, *"in no one in Israel have I found such faith."* Needless to say the man's servant was healed.

What a fitting response for us to make as we prepare to receive the body and blood of the Lord. What's even more interesting is that this man wasn't even among the people of

Israel. He was the enemy. He was one of the occupying Romans. As a Roman, he didn't care about the Jewish people or their religious beliefs. He was a pagan. But somehow, he came to have faith in Jesus. And what a faith he had! Such a faith that even Jesus marveled. Can you imagine doing something that makes Jesus amazed?

The truth is all this man did was believe that Jesus had the power to heal his servant. He then let his faith in Jesus take charge of everything else. This powerful Roman commander who had one hundred men under his authority recognized that Jesus had the authority to heal his servant, even by his word alone. What's even more amazing is that he humbled himself by declaring that he wasn't worthy to have Jesus (a poor Jewish son of a carpenter) enter into his house. When you mix great faith and great humility what you get is a great saint. That should be what we all strive for, all the time, but especially as we prepare to receive Jesus in the Eucharist. It takes great faith to believe that what looks, feels, and tastes like bread, is actually the body, blood, soul and divinity of Jesus. It also takes great humility to recognize that no matter how great we may be in the world's eyes or even our own, ultimately, all of our best efforts do not produce within us the righteousness to deserve Jesus. He is a gift to us. His grace is the result of his unending love for us. He loves us despite our weaknesses and sins. He loves us despite the cost to himself. And he offers himself to us here in the sacrament.

May we never take that for granted. May we never just go through the motions. May we always remember to humble ourselves before him. And most importantly, may we always approach Him with great faith to recognize his true presence.

As the Communion time begins, you may notice some people receive in different ways. Most people will take Communion in the hand, but there will be some who have the priest put the host directly on their tongue. Some will even kneel in front of the priest and receive on the tongue. There are many reasons for these variations. Basically, the idea is that many people feel that receiving on the tongue keeps their hands from touching Jesus, which they believe symbolizes their sin. For some, it's more reverent and pure to have the priest, whose hands have been ritually purified, place the host directly on their tongue. For other people, kneeling seems more humbling. Others are content to carefully receive the Eucharist in their hand. As you approach the priest, he will say, *"The body of Christ."* You will respond, *"Amen"*. Some people make the sign of the cross. Some will kneel and pray. Others will quietly make their way back to their seat. At this point, you may kneel or sit. It's up to you.

You may notice that not everybody goes forward to receive the Eucharist. That shouldn't surprise you since, as a convert, you probably spent many Masses sitting in your pew while everyone else was receiving. There are probably non-Catholics or perhaps Catholics who aren't in a place where they can receive, because they need to go to confession first. Either way, it's really nothing you need to worry about.

After you make it back to your pew, you can either sit or kneel and pray until everyone is finished receiving. I'm sure it may seem weird to people if they see me, but I often kneel while I watch others go forward. Why would I do that? It's because I am so grateful for my new family. I pray for them. I watch them and I think, *That guy's Catholic, those kids are Catholic! She's a Catholic too! What an amazing and diverse family we all are.* Maybe I will get over that someday, but for now it's just what I do. I'm so proud to be part of this Church. If I wasn't so reserved, I would probably stand in the aisle and high-five everyone after they received. *That's right! You did it! Give me some! Who's the Catholic? This guy is!!!*

Yeah, I probably shouldn't do that.

As the Mass ends, the priest will close with a prayer and offer the final blessing. As we make the sign of the cross, we seal everything we have just participated in under the sign of the Trinity. This always makes me feel empowered and thankful. It's as if my soul and body have been cleansed and infused with new life and grace. I often think of the time when Jesus told the crowds, *"Those who eat my flesh and drink my blood abide in me, and I in them." (John 6:56).*

Later in John 15, as Jesus was preparing to institute the Eucharist (where all of this would be tied together), Jesus told the disciples, *"I am the vine, you are the branches. Those who abide in me and I in them bear much fruit, because apart from me you can do nothing." (John 15:5).*

Abiding in Jesus has always been something that mattered to me, long before I became Catholic. Often much of what it meant to "abide" in Jesus meant having faith and keeping His commands to *"love one another as I have loved you" (John 15:12).* None of that has changed for me as a Catholic, but now I feel as if I am receiving the fullness of what Jesus offers us. Is it possible to be a Christian without being a Catholic? Of course it is, but as you are learning now, the Catholic faith brings more to the altar than symbols and memorials. The Church brings Jesus to us in a way that we've never experienced before. In Catholicism, there is recognition of the ways God brings the supernatural to us through the natural. As a convert, a lot of that is going to seem strange and maybe even a little superstitious. How can this piece of bread become the body of Jesus? Why do people freak out if a little piece breaks off and falls to the floor? Do I really need holy water sprinkled on me?

In my former churches it puzzled me that, on one hand, we had some of the ritualistic elements around Communion, but it didn't really make sense to me since it was only viewed as a memorial meal. For example, only ordained or licensed pastors were technically allowed to celebrate Communion, but I never really understood why. If it's just a memorial meal, then what's the big deal? Sometimes people would treat the bread and grape juice with reverence and respect, but after it was over it would just get thrown in the trash and dumped down the drain. If it's only a symbol, then does it really matter?

The way Protestant churches view Communion is complicated. Even the Reformers couldn't agree on what to do with Communion after they broke away from the Catholic Church in the sixteenth century. Most mainline denominations refer to it as a sacrament, but other Evangelical groups call it an ordinance. I never really understood the difference. Depending on where you have converted from, it may take some time to get used to having Communion every Mass. We celebrated Communion once a month in the United Methodist Church. That meant the sermon had to be about ten minutes shorter, plus we needed an extra song or two to fill the time. In other churches I've attended, Communion was held just a handful of times throughout the year. Maybe your experience was different.

One of my friends pastors a Protestant church where they serve Communion every week, so I know that it does happen, but I think they are in the minority.

As a Catholic, the Eucharist is now the most important thing you experience, not just in the Mass, but in life itself. This may be an adjustment for you in your first year in the Church, but I want to encourage you to approach Jesus in the Eucharist with humility, faith, and obedience every time. You will see amazing things happen. The supernatural God comes into the natural world, right there on the altar, and then you and I get to receive Him not just into our hearts, but into our bodies. It's beyond incredible. This is why daily Mass exists. Once you recognize the grace that comes to you from the Eucharist, you won't be able to get enough of it. It satisfies you in a way that you likely never experienced before.

> *"Jesus said to them, "I am the bread of life. Whoever comes to me will never be hungry, and whoever believes in me will never be thirsty."*
>
> *(John 6:35)*

Chapter 7

The Sacraments of Reconciliation and Marriage

What you need to know, what you need to do, what you need to not do

In the spring of 2017, I had finally made the difficult decision to resign my job at the church and convert to Catholicism. I had some practical challenges. The normal way people convert into the Church is through enrolling in a months-long process called RCIA (Rite of Christian Initiation of Adults). This is a course that meets weekly and helps people prepare to enter into the Church. The entire class officially enters the Church on the Easter Vigil. Its been this way for many years. However, exceptions can be made in certain circumstances. Thankfully for me, I have a priest who was willing to work with me. RCIA was not in the cards for me. In addition to my full-time job at First United Methodist Church, I also worked with Estelle at our photography studio. Between church meetings, youth group, and taking senior pictures, every night was booked solid.

I had been meeting with Fr. Chris every Tuesday morning for months. I had told him I was ready to convert and he agreed to walk me through the process himself. He knew that I had spent years studying the faith, so we didn't spend too much time covering the basics. He gave me some Scott Hahn teaching videos to watch (he still looks like my dad) and I would come in and we would talk about them. Mostly Fr. Chris was trying to help me discern whether or not I was really ready to do this. These meetings were the highlight of my week. All around me was uncertainty, anxiety, and fear. The walk down the hall into the other world of Fr. Chris's study led to a place I felt safe and secure. At the same time, Estelle and I were clinging to our faith, and each other, trusting that if God was truly calling us, we would be OK. Converting to Catholicism is a big deal no matter what your circumstances are, but when you're a pastor the stakes are raised a bit.

How would we live? Would we be able to earn enough with photography alone to pay our bills? On paper, the numbers painted a scary picture, but if this was what God was calling us to do then how could we refuse? Once the decision was made, I was cruising toward my resignation date of August 31. All was ready, but there were a few items that needed attention and they both involved the sacraments.

The Sacraments

What is a sacrament?

Depending on what type of Protestant church you came from, you may either know quite a lot about sacraments or absolutely nothing. A sacrament is defined as "an outward and visible sign of the hidden reality of salvation." Here's a passage from the <u>Catechism of the Catholic Church</u> that describes them:

> *"The seven sacraments are the signs and instruments*
> *by which the Holy Spirit spreads the grace of Christ,*
> *the head throughout the Church, which is His body"*
> *(CCC 774).*

Protestants and Catholics differ on the number of and nature of the sacraments. The Catholic Church recognizes seven sacraments: Baptism, Confirmation, the Eucharist, Marriage, Confession, Holy orders, and Anointing of the sick (Extreme unction).

In some Protestant churches there are three sacraments (Baptism, Communion, and Marriage). In others, Marriage is not considered a sacrament. In still others, the word "sacrament" has been substituted with "ordinance." This means they believed Christ "ordained" certain things, but they differ so substantially in their actual function and nature from Catholicism that they don't want there to be any confusing them with what those crazy Catholics believe. As expected, variations in doctrine and practice among Protestant churches are major. But one thing that separates many of them from Catholicism is the idea that the sacraments actually transmit grace. The sacraments don't merely signify grace, they *infuse* grace. I don't mean to get too technical here, but this is incredibly important for converts to grasp. One of the key aspects of Catholicism is its understanding of the sacraments.

Who is in charge of the sacraments?

Ultimately the answer is God. God himself dispenses grace through whatever means he wishes. The sacraments are the pathways God has created to bring his grace to us, depending on our situation. The Church understands its role as the vessel of grace by which God interacts with the world. The sacraments are where the grace of God and the people of God meet. It's the job of the Church to facilitate that. This is a job the Church takes very seriously, because it came directly from Jesus. Jesus is the one who gave his authority to his apostles (and their successors, the bishops). He didn't do this to give them the ability to have power and control over people but rather to serve them. The sacraments are a great gift to us and so is the Church, as dispenser and guardian of those sacraments.

Because the Church cares about the souls of its people, and about the integrity of the sacraments, great care is taken to ensure that the sacraments are handled correctly.

When someone converts to Catholicism, the Church sets in motion their relationship with the sacraments. Out of the seven, the two I want to focus on are Reconciliation (Confession) and Marriage.

A word for converts about baptism:

If you weren't baptized in the Trinitarian formula before you decided to become a Catholic, you will be on the day you enter the Church. Some people are surprised to discover that the Catholic Church accepts as valid any water baptism performed "In the name of the Father, and of the Son, and of the Holy Spirit." The reason for this is that even though the Church understands its role as the transmitter of grace through the sacraments, it is understood that God himself is the giver of all grace and is not bound exclusively to the sacraments performed in the Catholic Church, provided they are performed according to the valid form.

When my son Jesse was five and decided to baptize himself in the water fountain in the church hallway because he was too shy to stand in front of the church, it didn't quite meet the criteria. "It's OK, Mom," he told Estelle, "I've got preacher blood flowing through my veins." Nevertheless, we still baptized him in the church later.

If you were baptized, the priest may ask you for proof of your baptism at some point. He probably won't just take your word for it. Most churches will have a record somewhere. I had to do a little digging to find mine, but it was there.

A word for converts about confirmation:

I was confirmed in the United Methodist Church when I was in seventh grade, because that's what seventh graders did. After the yearlong cycle of our Sunday morning class, the group of us stood in front of the church and made vows that we actually believed the stuff we learned about Jesus, therefore "confirming" our baptism. We also vowed to be faithful members of the United Methodist Church. Next, we had a group photo taken, which was framed and hung on the wall in the church hallway (where it will hang for all eternity). And that was it! Most of the kids in my confirmation class never came back to church again.

Sadly, this was the same scenario I saw play out year after year, even in my last church. Confirmation might as well be called, "The last thing 80 percent of us ever do here." To me, and also to the senior pastor, this was tragic. Why in the world would people go through a process to learn what it means to be a faithful disciple of Jesus and a good church member, only to let that serve as more of a graduation from church rather than an entrance into the fullness of it?

When you convert to Roman Catholicism, your baptism doesn't need to be repeated, but you will receive the Sacrament of Confirmation. This is when you profess your belief in the faith and promise to be obedient to the divinely revealed teaching of the Church.

Reconciliation

What You Need to Know

Independence Day 2017 was a Tuesday. I had the day off from the Methodist Church, but Fr. Chris and I still met. I was becoming more and more anxious. My days at the Methodist Church were becoming difficult. I had announced my resignation but I was still there until the end of August. That was tough because people felt like I had rejected them. They didn't understand why I was doing this. Things were going great at our local church, even though the denomination was in chaos. We were preparing to break ground on a $9-million facility on twenty-five acres on the edge of town. This was the fulfillment of years of planning, praying, and fund-raising. I had been a big part of so many things there. More difficult was the fact that the relationships we had there would never be the same. Being a pastor is a demanding job for many reasons, but when you're a part of a great local church, it's also very fulfilling. That was my situation, and I was leaving it. Most people were gracious and supportive, but also brokenhearted. I did get some off-handed comments from people here and there about how they once read a book that said the pope was the anti-Christ, but I didn't deal with too many anti-Catholic comments, (at least none made to my face).

Estelle and I were doing well. We were both ready to see what God would do, but there was stress. I am so thankful that I'm married to a woman who has supported me in all this. This wasn't her idea. She wasn't the one having a crisis of faith. She was perfectly content to stay where we were. A lot of people have asked Estelle how she handled it. She always tells them, "it's tough, but if this is what God is calling my husband to do, then I am right there with him." I can't overstate how important Estelle's support has been to me. I am so grateful. I know of many pastors whose wives are the complete opposite. I heard a story of a man whose wife threatened suicide if he decided to convert. I can't imagine.

In the midst of everything, I was facing major anxiety over something I knew was part of this conversion process, my first confession, the Sacrament of Reconciliation.

The Sacrament of Reconciliation is decidedly Catholic. I am unaware of any other church that believes or practices anything close to what the Catholic Church does when it comes to the Sacrament of Reconciliation. That's not to say other Christians don't confess their sins. James 5:16 says, *"Therefore confess your sins to one another, and pray for one another, so that you may be healed."*

Many men I know have "accountability partners," or something similar. The basic idea is that two individuals, or a small group of trusted friends, meet together to hear about each other's struggles and sins. They help each other grow in their holiness. Or people may meet with a pastor or therapist to reveal their sins. As helpful as these things are, there is no real comparison to what happens in Reconciliation. That's because this isn't just about telling your sins to the priest. You can actually do that and have it not be a sacrament. What happens during Reconciliation concludes with the priest giving *absolution* to the sinner. Absolution is the distinguishing factor, and only a Catholic priest is authorized to give it. When I was a Protestant, I would go crazy when a Catholic would say something like that. "Only Jesus can forgive sins," I would say. After all, doesn't Jesus himself say that? *"The Son of Man has authority on earth to forgive sins" (Luke 5:17–26).*

No Catholic would argue that, but we also have to deal with what Jesus does in John 20. The resurrected Jesus appeared to his disciples, breathed on them, and said, ...

> *"Receive the Holy Spirit. If you forgive the sins of any they are forgiven; if you retain the sins of any, they are retained"*
>
> *(John 20:22-23).*

The stock Protestant interpretation of these verses goes something like this: "Forgiving sins" is code for "preaching the gospel." If people hear the gospel and become Christians, they have their sins forgiven. If they hear the gospel and don't believe, they don't.

There are probably other interpretations out there (there always are), but this one seems to be the easiest to find. In my opinion, it doesn't hold water. What we see here in this text is a clear instance of Jesus giving his authority to forgive sins to the apostles.

That's what happens in the Sacrament of Reconciliation. So why do people get so offended at this? After giving a talk in a Catholic parish, a man approached me and said, "I used to be Catholic, but I left. Do you really think you have to tell your sins to a priest?" My answer to him was not a theological manifesto. I simply said, "I've never thought of it like that. I don't think about it in terms of what I *have* to do, I think of it more as what I *get* to do. If anybody *has* to do anything, it's the priest. He *has* to offer me absolution! Jesus Christ himself has made a way for his forgiving grace to be really and actually given to you in person, through one of his chosen servants. Why wouldn't you want that?" I asked. "I've never thought of it like that before," he replied.

I think often what people get hung up on is what they feel they have to do when it comes to the Sacrament of Reconciliation. We rarely think of it in terms of what we receive. If I gave you a check for $1 million, would you complain that you had to take it to the bank and give it to the teller so it could go into your account? Or would you be so grateful that you would run right to the bank, smile at the teller, and say, "Thank you so much"?

Fr. Chris says of confession, "It's the only sacrament where after receiving it you can physically feel differently." He's right (although he doesn't know what it feels like to be married). That's because when we enter into the confessional, we are carrying the hurt, guilt, and shame of our sins. When we leave, we are forgiven. We are freed. Jesus said so himself!

This freedom was something I had been looking forward to desperately. Even though I was a pastor, I was no stranger to sin. Like everyone, I had and still have areas of my life in which I have failed miserably. Many of these sins were embarrassing, humiliating, and not the kind of thing I wanted my priest to know about. This was causing me some pretty heavy anxiety. Even though I didn't have a date set for my first confession, I knew it was coming sooner or later and I was sweating it. I even looked up videos on YouTube about what it's like as an adult to make a first confession. How was I supposed to remember everything? What if I missed something? And even worse, what if when he hears it, he kicks me out? The rational part of me knew it was all going to be fine, but I was a mess. As I was sharing with Fr. Chris my struggles, he said, "Well, Keith, maybe you should just get this done soon." (Remember, at this point I wasn't Catholic.)

I said, "Yeah, I guess so." He then crossed himself and said, "In the name of the Father, and of the Son and of the Holy Spirit." My first confession was about to begin whether I was ready or not.

I don't know how every priest handles situations like this, but I am so grateful for Fr. Chris. He helped me through this every step of the way. When I would get stuck in a story or a detail, he would help me along. He would ask me questions with yes or no answers. He didn't pry. He didn't make me elaborate. He was fine with categories and general statements and didn't make me feel like I had to recount things in great detail. He told me that later there may be some specific things I would remember that I may want to bring back, and that would be OK. He handled it like a pro. He never reacted emotionally or seemed shocked at anything I said. After I was done, he led me in the Act of Contrition prayer, gave me absolution, and then said four words that freed me from so much shame: *Your sins are gone.*

For my penance I said ten Hail Marys. I felt like a huge weight was lifted. Independence Day indeed.

What You Need to Do

Go to confession at least monthly or when you know you have sinned.

There's no magic number when it comes to the frequency of going to confession. The *Catechism* mandates that confession be made at least once a year. That's the absolute minimum. How often you go to confession is up to you, but I recommend going at least once a month. Maybe you should go more frequently. Pope St. John Paul II, for example, went to confession weekly. I doubt many of us are more holy than he was. The idea is to make going to confession part of the rhythm of your life. It should be a regular practice. Making a standing appointment on your calendar will help you to maintain a healthy relationship with this sacrament. In instances when you know you have sinned gravely, get to confession as soon as you possibly can. Many churches offer confession before every Mass. This is great because it's not awesome sitting in Mass knowing you're not able to receive the Eucharist. Remember, it is a serious sin to receive the Eucharist while knowingly in a state of mortal sin. If you worry that you are bothering the priest by going to confession too often, err on the side of going too often. He will guide you.

Decide how you prefer to confess.

I have seen many scenes in movies depicting confession. None of them looked like what I experienced. In the movies, confession happens in a small wooden booth. The silhouetted priest is shielded behind a screen. The person enters and kneels and it begins. Often it's depicted as very impersonal and sterile. The person says their obligatory, "Bless me, Father, for I have sinned," and off they go.

Confession is sometimes exactly like that. Sometimes it's nice to enter a small box and spill your guts to someone who isn't looking at you. Other times people find it helpful to sit with their priest face-to-face.

My first confession took place in Fr. Chris's office, the same office where we met weekly. It wasn't anything like what I expected. I don't always do it that way, but if I see Fr. Chris and need to receive the Sacrament of Reconciliation, he doesn't say, "OK, let's meet in the confessional booth." I've even seen Fr. Chris hearing confessions outside in the parking lot with guys on their way to work, after our Tuesday morning men's meeting. The point is you can decide what's best for you when it comes to confession. Whether you sit behind a screen in the confessional or meet face-to-face with your priest, you need to make it a regular part of your life.

Tell the truth. Be direct.

For many of us, admitting our guilt is tough. Even though we know we have sinned, deep down the temptation to blame others or make excuses is always there. It makes sense. How many times have you heard things like, "What do you have to say for yourself?" "Tell me why you know what you did was wrong"? Or even, "I am waiting for a good explanation for your behavior."

In life, it's normal to have to explain your mess-ups, mistakes, and bad behavior. It's part of what we as humans do to each other. When someone sins against us, we want to hear an apology, but not just an apology; we want an explanation, a reason. We have come to expect that when we are in trouble, a simple "I'm sorry" rarely cuts it.

As a new Catholic, you may expect confession to be like that. It's not. Your priest isn't supposed to grill you. Don't feel the need to offer long explanations, tell stories, or make excuses. Just name your sins. God knows the situation. God knows what other people did. God even knows why you did what you did. Confession isn't about explaining your sin, it's about owning it and being sorry. Just confess it directly. Tell the truth. Don't withhold anything. Knowingly withholding sins you have committed since your last confession invalidates the whole thing. Just get it out and let it go.

Know that you are forgiven!

The point of confession is to receive absolution. Absolution means that your sins are gone. God no longer holds them against you. They have been removed from you "as far as the east is from the west" (Psalm 103:12). You have been cleansed by the Blood of the Lamb! You are free. Don't let yourself feel condemned any longer. God accepts the contrite person. God is faithful to forgive us! However, being forgiven by God doesn't mean there aren't some earthly consequences. Sin rarely involves only ourselves. There's usually someone else affected by it. God can forgive us but He doesn't cause time to travel backward and remove what we have done from history. One of the reasons why God hates sin so much is because of the damage it does to his children. Even after God forgives us, we still may need to do something to (if possible) repair the damage done to others. If I steal fifty dollars from my friend, and then go to confession, God can forgive me. But if I'm really sorry for what I've done, I will pay my friend back the fifty dollars. Paying back the money shouldn't make me feel unforgiven by God. If anything, I should be grateful that something I did to hurt another person could be restored. Not all sins against others can be fixed so easily.

Even after receiving absolution, the earthly consequences of our sins remain, as do what are called "temporal punishments." The nature of a temporal punishment is best understood this way: Sin is about more than something we do. Sin is also about our "unhealthy attachments" (CCC 1031). We can be forgiven of the eternal punishment our sins deserve, but what God is really interested in is our actually becoming holy. Jesus' words in the Gospel explain,

> [35]*"and one of them, a lawyer, asked him a question to test him.* [36]*"Teacher, which commandment in the law is the greatest?"* [37]*He said to him, "'You shall love the Lord your God with all your heart, and with*

all your soul, and with all your mind.' [38]*This is the greatest and first commandment.* [39]*And a second is like it: 'You shall love your neighbor as yourself.'* [40]*On these two commandments hang all the law and the prophets."*

Matthew (22:35–40).

When we sin, we are basically failing in these commands, for we are loving something, or someone—usually ourselves—more than God. By nature, that's what sin is. The behaviors God calls sinful are the result of these unhealthy attachments. The eternal punishment for sin is eternal separation from God in hell. We are forgiven of this punishment when we receive absolution, but the removal of these unhealthy attachments requires some work. That work is called penance. Doing penance is not to be thought of as some sort of vindictive punishment by God. Remember, the eternal consequences of your sin have been forgiven; penance is what helps you break those unhealthy attractions so that you actually become less and less inclined to sin. Remember, penance is not some little punishment the priest gives you that will make your sin go away. Penance starts inwardly. Just as the outward fruit of love of self is sin, the outward fruit of penance are things like prayers, fasting, giving to the needy, and other acts of love toward others. These outward acts alone mean nothing though, if not coming from an inward sense of sorrow for sin and love for God.

As a convert, this is a lot to understand. Most Protestants don't think about the relationship between sin, forgiveness, consequences, and punishment this way. Most Protestant theology views sin differently. What you may be used to is the idea that when you accept Jesus as your personal Lord and

Savior, all of your sins have been completely forgiven, past, present, and in some cases, future. The concept of earthly consequences remains, but there is really no Protestant version of temporal punishment that is close to what Catholicism teaches. If you've asked God for forgiveness, then by virtue of the asking and belief in the saving work of Jesus on the cross, you are totally and completely forgiven. The other main difference is that in Catholicism, sin, grace, and community are all tied together. When a person mortally sins, he has not only broken fellowship with God, but also with the Church. The Sacrament of Reconciliation not only restores union with God, but also with the Church. This idea is unique to Catholicism from a theological point of view. Some Protestant churches exercise "church discipline," in which a person may receive some form of public chastisement from the congregation, but that can vary according to different beliefs and practices.

In your first year in the Church, you don't need to understand all the nuances. It will come to you. In the beginning of your life in the Church, what's important is knowing the power of confession and the amazing freedom God's forgiveness, exercised through a priest, brings.

What You Need to Not Do

Don't avoid it.

If you know you need to go to confession, just go. I've had plenty of moments where I thought, *I wonder if I should go to confession for that.* Sometimes I have been quick to go, other times I have put it off. I have never regretted going, but

I often regretted waiting. I know life is busy, but nothing is more important than having a right relationship with God and the Church. Again, having a standing appointment makes a great practice.

Don't worry about what your priest thinks of you.

I know you may find this hard to believe but your priest is a lot more worried about you when you haven't been to confession than when he sees you walk into confession again. It goes against so much of our experiences as converts, but the reality is this: it doesn't matter what your priest thinks of you. He's not there to give out medals for who is the most righteous. He's there to help his people save their souls.

Listen, he knows you're not perfect. You aren't going to shock him with anything you say. Chances are he has heard worse. Working in the church world as long as I did taught me that even among the most typical, normal, church folk are some deeply hurting people, many of whom are stuck in a pattern of sin or are full of shame for things they have done. Sin affects us all. None of us are perfect. Your priest knows that already. When you joined the Church he did not run to his bishop saying, "We've found the perfect person written about in St. Margarita's diary!" Most likely you and I are just like everyone else in his parish, a sinner. I remember feeling scared that Fr. Chris wouldn't want to be my friend if he heard my confession. I get it. We want people to like and respect us, and we never had to tell our previous pastor all of our deepest darkest sins. It's tough to open yourself up to that kind of vulnerability. Here's what you need to know: it really doesn't matter if your priest is your friend. He's not there to be your *friend.* He's there to be your *priest.* It's great if he becomes your friend, but that's not his main concern when it comes to you. It shouldn't be yours either. Think of him more as a physician and less like a buddy. Your physician has intimate knowledge of you (depending on your age, VERY intimate knowledge). You may like him or her as a person, but you wouldn't tell them "no" if at your doctor's appointment they asked you to drop your pants, turn to the left, and cough. (Women have a whole other thing happening here.) The reason is because that's the purpose of the relationship. Refusing to cooperate with your doctor when they want to examine your physical body because you are afraid of what they would think of you sounds ridiculous. The same is true for your priest. When he is helping you to examine your soul, let him do his job. Don't worry about what he thinks. He isn't worried about it. If you're concerned about confidentiality, remember, your priest has taken a very serious oath not to divulge anything you tell him in confession. He is not to use any of the information against you in any way. This is an oath that you can trust.

What you will undoubtedly experience is that your priest will treat you just the same as he did before he heard your confession. He's not giving you the stink-eye when you walk into the church. He's not disappointed because he was secretly hoping you were the first sinless person who joined his church. If you make your confession in the booth behind a screen, he might not even know who you are. Remember, he hears lots of confessions, not only yours. You are just one of many. You aren't special. What a relief!

Marriage

What You Need to Know

One of the first things that married converts have to deal with is how their marriage is viewed by the Church. The Church does not accept all marriages to be sacramentally valid. For many people, this is a deal breaker for their conversion. In a society where the definition of marriage is being debated, even among Christians, and is often a completely secular legal arrangement, we have to ask ourselves as Christians, "Is marriage a sacrament?" And if it is, then who is in charge of sacraments? The answer to the first question for virtually all Christians is that yes, marriage is a sacrament. It's the answer to the second question that sometimes throws people off. When it comes to marriage, this can be dicey for converts. Not all churches have the same view of marriage and sometimes married converts are shocked to discover that their marriage isn't recognized as sacramentally valid by the Catholic Church. I get it. That can feel like a punch in the gut.

I've talked to a few people who abandoned the conversion process because of the ramifications it would have on their marriage. It's tough. Estelle and I have been there. It was hard to learn that because of our decision not to marry in the Catholic Church and without permission from her priest (Estelle was baptized and raised Catholic), our twenty-one-year marriage wasn't sacramentally valid in the eyes of the Church. When I first heard that back in my early explorations of Catholicism, it was just the thing I needed to hear to send me packing. At that point, I had been considering the claims of the Church and found myself drawn to the Eucharist. I was still not ready to accept the authority of the Church, and this was the issue that made me stop and run away. *How can these guys say I am not really married? What gives them the right?* I angrily stormed out of the priest's office and never talked to him again (until last year when I spoke in his church about my conversion).

What I've come to realize is that it all comes down to the issue of authority. When I wasn't ready to accept the authority of the Church, I ran away in rebellion. Years later when I was ready to accept the authority, I went to the church and simply said, "How do we fix this?"

It turns out it was not that big a deal. We simply got married in the Church one day with some good friends standing by our sides. It wasn't a situation where we felt like it was a forced thing. It was a gift! It was an opportunity to have our marriage blessed in a way we never experienced before. I know for some people it's not as easy. If someone has been married before and the relationship ended, the Church needs to make sure there isn't a situation going on where someone is actually still married to another person. Just because a civil judge says someone is divorced doesn't mean that God accepts that.

Consequently, just because a judge, or even a pastor, says someone is married doesn't mean that God accepts that either. I know that runs contrary to what many people think about marriage and divorce, but what we must remember is that as Christians we believe marriage was instituted by God. The words of Jesus spell it out clearly when He said about marriage,

"...what God has joined together, let no one separate."
(Matthew19:6).

When someone who has been married and divorced and is now married again wants to convert to Catholicism, the issue of their first marriage needs to be addressed. The Church may choose to look into the situation to determine whether or not the first marriage was actually valid in the first place. If it was, then there are some tough choices ahead. If it wasn't, then the Church can declare the first marriage invalid (annulled), and the individuals can proceed with getting their current marriage con-validated (blessed and made valid) by the Church, if necessary.

It may seem like a lot of hoops to jump through, but as I have told people personally, if you really believe the Catholic Church to be the fullness of the faith and possessing the authority of Jesus, then you have to make the choice to submit all of yourself, and your marriage, to the authority of the Church. Otherwise, what's the point?

Converting to Catholicism isn't like switching churches because you like the music better or because you moved. Few Protestants these days have the kind of relationship with their church that demands the type of obedience and submission found in Catholicism. Sure, there are multitudes who disobey the Catholic Church every day and still call themselves practicing Catholics. That doesn't justify anything. When a person converts, they stand before the congregation and declare that they believe everything the Church teaches to be revealed by God. That includes the Church's teaching about marriage. Converts are saying that they recognize a divine authority has been given to the Church, and they wish to submit themselves to it. This concept doesn't really exist in the Protestant world in the same way. Yes, there are exceptions. There are churches who claim that type of authority over their members, but they have no historical or scriptural basis for it. For most Protestants, if they don't like what a particular church teaches, they can simply leave and find another one.

The bottom line is this: bring your marriage under the authority of the Church, no matter how tough it is, and you will find grace and healing. Estelle and I did that. I'm not holding us up as perfect because we are far from it. It took years before I would consider that. Now that it's done, we are so blessed that we did.

What You Need to Do

Tell your priest your situation right away.

Depending on the circumstances, even if you weren't married in a Catholic Church, your marriage could still be valid. If neither spouse was Catholic or married before, and you were married by a pastor under the standard Trinitarian form (Father, Son, and Holy Spirit) your marriage is probably valid. If neither of you were married before and it wasn't performed that way, a simple service in your church will take care of it. If there are previous marriages involved, that is a more complicated situation. Have your priest advise you as to what needs to be done right away.

Patiently work through the necessary steps.

Whatever the situation is, you are better off working through it than running away from it. The reason this is all such a big deal is because you could be in serious sin and not even realize it. Bringing the situation into the light may cause some practical issues, but whatever they are is better than living in a state of serious sin. It may seem overwhelming and at times it may feel as if it's too much to deal with. It can be tempting to bail on your conversion. Just be patient and work through it. God gives grace to the humble. You are sowing seeds of faith and obedience that will reap a harvest once you get through this part of the process. Don't give up!

Offer your struggles to Jesus as a sacrifice.

You don't have to hide your pain and frustrations from Jesus. You don't have to put on a happy face and act like everything is OK. The fact is, it's going to be OK. It's going to be better than OK. Whenever we bring a new area of our lives into submission to God's will, there is often a time of intense struggle. It's OK to be real about that with your priest and especially with Jesus. Let this struggle cause you to run to Jesus, not away from him. Go to him in prayer and give him your pain.

> *"Cast all your anxiety on him, because he cares for you"*
> *(1 Peter 5:7).*

You just may be amazed at what happens when you refuse to let anything stand in the way of your obedience to Jesus and his Church. Graces will flow as you offer the situation to him.

Love your spouse in the ways you can.

If you do find yourself in a situation where the Church has said your current marriage needs to be con-validated, there will be some things that are impacted immediately. You should not have sexual relations with each other until this is resolved. I know that may seem crazy since you may have been civilly "married" for a while (over two decades in my case). Try not to freak out. The sacrifices you make to do this right will reap rewards. Think of this whole season as an example of what St. Paul taught when he said,

> *"Do not deprive one another except perhaps by agreement for a set time, to devote yourselves to prayer,"*
> *(1 Corinthians 7:5).*

Just because you can't have sex doesn't mean you have to treat each other like strangers. You are still in love and are basically "engaged." Make some fun out of that! Date each other again like you did when you first met. Find other ways to show love to each other that don't end up with sex. It will seem strange, but it will also help you in your marriage.

If it's helpful, look at it as a fresh start. I made many mistakes in my marriage before converting to Catholicism. When I found out Estelle and I would be getting married in the Church, I took it as a chance to start fresh. I had often wished I could go back and do things differently. Even though I couldn't step into a time machine, I felt as if I had been given another chance. This time as a Catholic, married in the Church with its sacramental blessing, things could be better than ever. We decided to go for it. We offered ourselves and our marriage to God in a new way and the results have been amazing.

I don't know what your situation is. Maybe your marriage is a disaster, and when you found out it wasn't valid in the Church, you saw it as a way out. I'm not here to tell you how to handle that. If there are children involved, things aren't as simple as two adults deciding to break up. This is why you need to talk to your priest right away. Get some help. Many people have been, and are, in the same situation. Find some people you can talk to. Cover everything in prayer.

What You Need to Not Do

Don't refuse to obey the teaching of the Church.

It can be tempting to just quit. Don't do it. Your decision to become Catholic affects areas of your life you never expected, but that's a good thing! Remember the old platitude, "Jesus is Lord of everything or He is Lord of nothing." He's worthy of your obedience.

> *"All things work together for the good to those who love God and are called according to His purposes"*
> *(Romans 8:28).*

This verse is for you. You are doing this because you love God. Jesus said,

> *"If you love me, you will keep my commandments"*
> *(John 14:15).*

This is all about loving God. He will work it out. Don't quit.

Don't forget why you are doing this.

This is all about making your marriage the best it can be. Don't forget that. Think of this as investing for the future. You suffer for a little while, but in the end it will pay massive dividends. This is about loving your family more than you ever imagined, because although there are difficulties for now, you are opening an incredible channel of grace. Remember, marriage is a sacrament. That means God uses it to bring grace to us. He is faithful and will do his part. Never forget that.

Great graces await you as you continue in this new relationship with the sacraments. Remember, the sacraments are God's channels of grace. The more you embrace them the more you will see your life change. More important, you will see yourself change. God's grace isn't something applied over us so we can go to Heaven instead of hell when we die. God's grace is applied into us, so we actually change. God's grace through the sacraments works in and through us, conforming us more and more into the likeness of Jesus. It's hard work sometimes, but it's worth it!

> [11] *"For the grace of God has appeared, bringing salvation to all,* [12] *training us to renounce impiety and worldly passions, and in the present age to live lives that are self-controlled, upright, and godly"*
> *(Titus 2:11–12).*

> *"As we work together with him, we urge you also not to accept the grace of God in vain."*
> *(2 Corinthians 6:1).*

Chapter 8

Beads, Books, and Brethren

Tools for growth in the first year

What You Need to Know

Beads

The first time I actually heard people praying the Rosary, I was on a bus with thirty Catholics headed for a place in Bosnia where the Virgin Mary was supposedly appearing to some kids. I was nowhere near ready to become a Catholic. So what was I doing there?

My friend (and theological nemesis) Devin had invited me one day to meet a friend of his for lunch. He said it was very important. We went to my favorite Chinese restaurant and settled into the dining room. The buffet was stocked and I was starving. I had no idea what to expect from the meeting but this place had great wings. Devin's friend arrived and introduced himself to me, "I'm Greg, nice to meet you." Greg seemed like a nice guy. He looked to be about ten years older than me. He kind

of reminded me of a cleaner-looking version of the actor that
played one of the criminals in *Home Alone*. Not Joe Pesci, the
other guy. It wasn't unusual for me to have lunch with people
I was meeting for the first time. When you're in ministry, you
have a lot of lunch meetings. People want to talk about your
church (or more often *their* church), or pick your brain about
some aspect of ministry. I wondered if this was why I was there.
I could tell that Greg was a Catholic because he crossed himself
before we prayed. Whenever I went to lunch with Devin, we
usually both had to pray before meals. He would gesture for
me to start and I would say something like, *"Lord Jesus, we
thank you for this day and this food, bless it to our bodies in
Jesus name. Amen."* Simple enough. Then Devin would recite
the typical Catholic prayer, *"Bless us, O Lord, and these Thy
gifts, which we are about to receive from Thy bounty through
Christ, our Lord. Amen."* (Not *Ay-men* like a normal person, but
AH-men.) OK, whatever, now we can eat.

"My daughter goes to your youth group," Greg said. I nearly
ran out of there. Greg is not a scary man, but he's a lot bigger
than I am. I immediately jumped to the conclusion that I was
in some kind of trouble. Devin was leading the youth ministry
across town at Holy Family Catholic Church and we had a sort
of friendly rivalry. Occasionally some of "my" students would
attend his youth ministry and sometimes "his" students would
attend mine. I always respected Devin and truly wanted his
youth ministry to succeed. Likewise, he did a lot to help me
and our youth ministry, beyond designing our first logo. But
when it came to "our" students, we were both overly protec-
tive. When Greg began by telling me his daughter attended
my youth ministry, I braced for him to harshly chastise me
for corrupting his daughter's Catholicism with my heretical

Protestant rock 'n' roll youth service. I couldn't have been more wrong. Greg thanked me for all I was doing to help his daughter grow in her faith. He explained that she had never been that excited about church, but each Wednesday night she couldn't wait to go to Pine St. High. He told me how she would come home and excitedly tell him and his wife, Sandi, all that happened that week. I was sure happy to hear that. I stuffed my face with crab rangoon dipped in just the right mixture of sweet and sour sauce and hot mustard as Greg explained to me why he wanted Devin to introduce us.

"Keith, I know this is going to sound crazy, but I want to invite you on an all-expense-paid trip to Europe."

I didn't expect *that*! What was this all about? Maybe Greg was one of those guys who liked to invite people to lunch, draw circles on napkins, and explain how they could make lots of money by becoming their own boss by starting their own "business." Needless to say, my guard was up.

Then Greg told me a story not unlike the one I first heard from Devin. It was a story about conversion to Christ resulting in a deep, personal, and passionate relationship with Jesus. Now I knew *two* Catholics who loved Jesus! Greg's conversion took place during a trip he took to a village in Bosnia-Herzegovina. The village was named Medjugorje, and people from all over the world went there because six kids claimed to have been receiving messages from the Virgin Mary since 1982. *What the???* The experience changed Greg so radically that he made it his personal mission to bring as many people as possible with him, as he would return once or twice each year. Even though Greg had never met me, he obviously knew I wasn't a Catholic, but for some reason I came into his mind as a person to invite. I needed a minute (and an egg roll) to process this.

When he mentioned this trip would include a visit to Italy (the land of my ancestry) and wouldn't cost me a dime, I thought to myself, *I can put up with all this wacky Catholic stuff if it means a free trip to Europe. Devin was going too, so at least I would know one other person. I'll just keep my head down and not worship any statues. Then again, maybe it's not a good idea.*

I cracked open the stale but always tasty fortune cookie, thanked him for the generous offer and for lunch. I promised I would give it some thought. The three of us looked at each other with wide eyes as I threw down my fortune on the table.

You will be going on an exciting journey.

* * *

Sitting on the bus preparing to depart on what would be a twenty-four-hour trip, I knew I was out of my element. Before the bus even left the parking lot of Our Lady of Victory Church, everyone was already rubbing their beads and reciting a prayer I had never heard before. *For the sake of His sorrowful passion, have mercy on us and on the whole world.*

Greg said the first part aloud himself, then everyone (except me) said the second part over and over. I kept thinking to myself, I wonder if this is what Jesus meant when he warned against praying "vain repetitions." The people didn't seem to be praying in vain. They wholeheartedly and dutifully said their responses. But the repetition thing was freaking me out. We hadn't even left the state and I was already wondering what I had gotten myself into.

On that trip I learned two things about Catholics that I didn't know before:

> 1. Catholics don't have hang-ups about drinking alcohol together, in moderation of course.
> 2. Catholics LOVE to pray.

Every day there were set times when everyone would pray the Rosary and the Chaplet of Divine Mercy. Not to mention these Catholics insisted on having Mass *every* day. I had never seen anything like that before. Some of the churches I attended in the past had church services on Sunday morning and Sunday evening. The really serious Christians also came for a Wednesday evening program and maybe another Bible study or small group. But a straight-up church service like the Mass every day? What was all of this?

As crazy as it seemed to me, it was amazing. I was completely caught off guard watching these people worship Jesus. They loved every minute of it. When it was time for Mass, the Rosary, or a holy hour, it was approached with the same level of excitement, or more, than when it was time to eat! Nobody treated it like it was a hassle or some religious duty they had to perform. They lived for this stuff. It was as if all of the prayers and devotions were the air they breathed. Either these people were a little nuts or I was missing something.

There were lots of things on that trip that caused me to rethink my view of the spiritual life of run-of-the-mill Catholics, but perhaps the most impactful was seeing their devotional life lived out. Even though I was a Protestant, I was always invited to participate in the prayers, Mass (not receiving the Eucharist), and everything else they did. I did my best, but I had some pretty major questions about so much of what was going on:

Why are all the prayers so programmed?
Shouldn't prayer be from the heart?
Why do Catholics pray to dead saints?
Isn't that a sin?
What's the deal with Adoration?"
Why do Catholics worship a piece of the Communion bread?
There's no way I am ever bowing down to a statue!
Haven't these guys ever read the Ten Commandments?

Eventually, these questions were all answered for me. I could write a book about each one (many others already have). When you become a Catholic, a whole new universe of devotional life is revealed. I was no stranger to devotions and quiet time as a Protestant, but I am amazed at how my first year in the Church showed me things I never imagined.

I can in no way give an exhaustive list of the devotional practices and prayers that are utilized by Catholics all over the world. It would take a lifetime to explore half of what is out there. The two-thousand-year-old Church has yielded countless devotions, prayers, and spiritual writings. It can be a little tough to figure out how to get started using them. Try not to get overwhelmed. You don't need to do everything. Sometimes at my men's group, guys will recommend certain chaplets, novenas, consecrations, and middle of the night holy hours. When I first joined, I felt like I needed to grab everything all at once. I quickly become overwhelmed. I couldn't keep up. What I've discovered is that when you take it slowly, these things will help you grow tremendously.

What You Need to Do

- Pray the Rosary daily.
- Spend at least an hour a week in Eucharistic Adoration.
- Fast from something every Friday.
- Attend a weekday Mass at least once a week.

Right now some Catholics are screaming at this book.

> *What about the Liturgy of the Hours?*
> *You forgot the St. Louis de Montfort Marian consecration!*
> *No Novenas???*
> *Why didn't you mention the brown scapular?*
> *Everyone needs a spiritual director!*

All of those things are awesome. You'll get there. Estelle and I recently started praying the Liturgy of the Hours (Morning and Night, at least) every day. It's amazing, but we had to work up to that. You have to start somewhere, but if you overcommit yourself in the beginning, you may get overwhelmed and revert back to doing very little.

This list was not handed down to me by St. Michael the Archangel. It's merely my suggestion of things that make a great start in your first year as a Catholic. If other things prove helpful to you, that's great! The point is this: take some of these new tools of devotion and use them. Your faith is about to explode! Let's jump in.

Pray the Rosary Daily

I love to listen to talks and sermons. When I'm mowing my lawn, editing photos, or riding my Harley, it's almost always done with earbuds and a sermon. I'm always on YouTube. Estelle told me the other day, "I got to see a couple of your YouTube searches when I went on your computer." "Prayers That Satan Hates" and "How to Clean a Leaky Snow Thrower Carburetor" were two that she mentioned. Sounds about right to me! When I was thinking about becoming a Catholic, I watched videos about apologetics constantly. Talks by men like Steve Ray, Scott Hahn, Dr. Taylor Marshall, and all the guys at Catholic Answers were just some of what I devoured. Slowly but surely, my objections to Catholicism were being answered.

Not long after I joined the Church, I was preparing to go on my weekly Sunday afternoon motorcycle ride. I was scrolling through YouTube looking for something to listen to on the ride. I decided it was time for a little break from the apologetics stuff; so instead, I pressed play on a talk by a man named Fr. Don Calloway entitled "The Rosary: Spiritual Sword of Our Lady." I had never listened to a talk about the Rosary before, but for some reason this seemed interesting. I threw on my boots and leather jacket, put my earbuds in, strapped on my helmet and hit the road. I'm sure anyone who saw me flying down the highway on my blacked-out Harley Sportster 48 would have never guessed I was listening to a talk about the Rosary.

This talk blew my mind. I knew next to nothing about the Rosary. I knew there were "mysteries" and I knew the prayers, but I had no idea where it all came from or what it was really about. When you become a Catholic, you can bet on somebody giving you a Rosary as a gift. I have several. What are you supposed to do with it? Is it a necklace? Is it a good-luck charm for your rearview mirror? For most of us converts, learning about the Rosary wasn't a requirement to join the Church. It's just sort of built into the fabric of Catholicism. I was ready to get answers.

Fr. Calloway's talk centered on the material in a book he had just released called *Champions of the Rosary*. In the talk, he outlined the history of the Rosary, as well as how evil spiritual forces over the years have tried to destroy it. There were some incredible stories. What caught my interest was the concept of the Rosary as a weapon against evil. Over and over, Fr. Calloway described miraculous events in which the Rosary had been used to defeat evil. It was like nothing I'd ever heard before.

I could certainly relate to what it felt like being in a spiritual battle. When I left my job at First United Methodist Church to become a Catholic, I also left behind a modest (but adequate) salary, health insurance, and retirement benefits. Our photography business was doing reasonably well, but the overall income we brought home after all our expenses was much less than what we were used to earning. What was more stressful was that running that type of business is tough because there are no guarantees. We've worked very hard to do the best work we can for our clients, but every year it feels like we start from scratch. Very few of our jobs are yearly repeats (unless some kid fails the twelfth grade and needs extra senior photos to document that) and, when the weather turns cold, we practically shut down. But 2017 was a decent year for our business and we were feeling OK, though we really had no assurance that it would continue. We had decided that whatever sacrifices we had to make in order to follow God on this journey would be well worth it. But that didn't mean it was easy. When it came to going to church, our family was in a tough spot too. As I've mentioned, our kids were of the age where it was determined we shouldn't force our Catholicism on them. We needed to let them own their faith and choose for themselves what they would do. Our son Jesse had graduated high school that year and immediately left for Basic Training for the National Guard, so he was gone. Our oldest is our daughter, Devon. At the time, she was twenty and working a summer internship at First United Methodist Church, which I had just left. Our youngest son, Drew, was a junior in high school and still very active at First United Methodist Church. At first, we tried taking them to Mass with us, but they had no real interest in it. We would often hear, "Just because you and mom became Catholic doesn't mean we have to." We understood and respected that, but it was hard not being together in church on Sunday mornings. Our family has always been very tight. We love being together. For Estelle especially, this was heartbreaking. She would often ask me things like, "Is this what God really wants? Why can't we all be together? How can we live like this?"

Perhaps the most difficult thing I was facing at that time was the reality that my mother was losing her battle with pancreatic cancer. Until her shocking diagnosis in December 2015, my mom was a healthy, vibrant woman, full of life and love for her family and her Lord. She and my father had the most amazing marriage anybody who knew them had ever seen. They had been married nearly fifty years and they still acted like teenagers around each other. We were all very close, and watching her suffer and fight was beyond awful. Endless trips to the Mayo Clinic for proton beam radiation and round after round of chemo completely wrecked her body, but mom was still fighting.

My close friend Ryan, who had also been diagnosed with cancer, wasn't doing well either, and then Estelle lost her grandmother, followed closely by the death of her uncle (and godfather) Mike. Our family was hurting. We needed each other, but now we were not even going to the same church.

It was tough being so excited about becoming Catholic then sitting in Mass without our kids. Sometimes Estelle would cry through the entire Mass. We knew God was in this, but it was a struggle. There were many layers of spiritual and emotional battles being fought all around and inside us. Sometimes it was exhausting just going to church. Estelle and I were clinging to each other and doing our best to hold it together, but this was more difficult than we expected. Often I felt helpless about what was going on around me. After all, this had been my decision. I was the one who couldn't just leave well enough alone and find a way to be happy in the United Methodist Church. All of this uncertainty and insecurity was the result of my choice. Was there anything I could do to make it better?

When Fr. Calloway spoke about the Rosary in terms of a weapon against evil, I was ready to pick it up and fight. I wanted so desperately to see God's power at work, and if the Rosary was half of what Fr. Calloway claimed it could be, I wanted to know about it. What I learned is the Rosary *is* a weapon, not a good-luck charm.

There are a lot of Catholics who treat some of these devotionals, especially the Rosary, like good-luck charms. Don't be misled. Simply having a Rosary in your pocket or hiding one in someone's car or underwear drawer doesn't scare the devil away. When I was a Protestant, I would hear stuff like that and roll my eyes. It simply fed into the misconception I had that Catholics were superstitious weirdos. I don't feel that same way about all Catholics anymore, but let's be honest—some Catholics *are* superstitious weirdos. Some *Protestants* are superstitious weirdos too. Why do you think guys like Peter Popoff can make millions selling Miracle Water or Dirt from Jerusalem on Christian TV?

Misusing devotional practices is not confined to a certain belief system. Everyone wants to find a way to manipulate their spiritual reality with the hope that it will change their material reality. In other words, we all want the magic formula that will fix everything we think is wrong with our lives. This was never the purpose behind the Rosary. There's nothing in Catholic teaching that suggests that if you pray the Rosary, all your problems will disappear. Critical to understanding the power of the Rosary is understanding what it's for and what it is.

At its simplest level, the Rosary is a tool for prayer. Woven into this prayer tool are the "mysteries" (Catholic word for "awesome stuff we need to deeply think about"). These mysteries take us on a journey of remembrance, celebration, and devotion as we consider key events in God's plan of salvation. The prayers that make up the rosary are the Our Father, the Hail Mary, the Glory Be, and the Hail, Holy Queen.

The power of these prayers comes from the fact that they have nothing to do with our lives and our problems. They are 100 percent focused on God. THIS is why it is such an effective weapon against evil. Praying the Rosary calibrates our focus and our hearts toward God and away from us. This is the kind of thing the devil hates.

When I was a Protestant, I would sometimes see Catholics praying the Rosary and think, *They are like robots*, mindlessly saying these words. *Vain repetitions,* I would think. Can that happen? Yes, but the problem Jesus had with the prayers of certain people wasn't the *repetition* part (the Psalms are repetitious at times), it had everything to do with the *vain* part.

So here's what you do: don't pray the Rosary in vain. Really mean it. Let your heart sink into it and use it as a way to focus yourself on God. Who cares what you sound like? It might come off to jerks, like I used to be, as "robotic" or whatever, but only you know what's going on in your heart. When truly prayed with devotion and love for God, this thing is powerful! Sometimes I like to imagine each bead as thrusting a sword into Satan's heart. Sometimes I think of the powerful prayers as building layers of protection around my family. Other times I get lost in the reality of each mystery. With all that was going on around us, I needed a weapon against evil. In the Rosary, I found one.

One of the most powerful experiences I've ever had with the Rosary came in October 2018 as Greg was leading a group of us up toward Cross Mountain in Medjugorje. There were seven of us, including Estelle and me, on this particular trip. Even though some of us had just met days earlier, we had all become fast friends. As we walked along the dirt path enjoying the beautiful day, it was easy for conversation and laughter to flow. Greg had a natural way of steering us toward the spiritual significance of what we were doing. He can be a pretty hilarious guy and loves to joke around, but he didn't bring all of us on this trip just to have some laughs and visit new places. Greg cares deeply about the spiritual lives of the people he chooses to bring on his trips and he wanted to make sure we didn't lose sight of what God wanted to do in our lives. As we walked, Greg invited us to pray the Sorrowful Mysteries. As we headed toward the base of the mountain, our hearts turned toward

Jesus. As Greg led us, he not only recited the first part of the prayers, he also described each of the mysteries in detail and invited us to truly consider what they meant.

The first sorrowful mystery is the Agony in the Garden. Imagine the scene. Jesus had just celebrated the Last Supper with his disciples and he knew that Judas had already betrayed him. While the disciples failed to stay awake, Jesus went alone to the Garden of Gethsemane. There, as he contemplated what was about to happen to him, his sorrow overwhelmed him so that he began to sweat drops of blood. All the while his disciples slept unaware. How have we been unaware of what our Lord has done for us? How have we slept through his sufferings for us? What great love he has for us! "Not my will, but yours be done," Jesus prayed to the Father, knowing the unspeakable suffering that would soon follow.

I wish I'd had a video camera to record that. It was unreal. Greg eloquently described each mystery while inviting us to pray the prayers that followed. As we ended with the Hail, Holy Queen, we reached the base of the mountain, but I felt as if I had already been to the top. We all did. That's why the Rosary is a weapon against evil.

You need to begin the practice of praying it every day. I don't know what works best for you. For me, if I wait until the end of the day, it doesn't work. I like to wake up early, and while the house is still quiet I will take my place on my sofa and pray, or sometimes I head to my man cave and pray in between sets of push-ups.

If I know I'm going to weekday Mass, I'll arrive early and pray with others who daily do the same. Finally, I regularly play a Gregorian Chant Latin version of the Rosary I found on (you guessed it) YouTube. That often serves as my background music when I'm in the studio working alone on photographs.

When I was first starting with the Rosary, I didn't know what I was doing. I downloaded an app on my iPhone and prayed along with it. There are tons of resources and, I guarantee, plenty of people in your parish who would love to teach you. Whatever your particular situation is, find a way to make this happen every day. You'll fail occasionally, but stick with it. Doing so will ensure your first year in the Church will be filled with grace. St. Padre Pio said, *"The Rosary is the weapon for these times."* Use the weapon!

Spend at least an hour a week in Eucharistic Adoration.

> [40] *"Then he came to the disciples and found them sleeping; and he said to Peter, "So, could you not stay awake with me one hour?* [41] *Stay awake and pray that you may not come into the time of trial; the spirit indeed is willing, but the flesh is weak."*
>
> *(Matthew 26:40-41).*

The clipboard was going around the room during one of our Tuesday morning men's group meetings. This was nothing surprising. Every week, at least one of the men in our group had a stack of flyers advertising something we were supposed to do. At first, I tried to jump in and participate in everything that was going on, but I quickly learned that was neither possible nor expected. The men who come to our group are a great mix of individuals. I love them all. They're serious about their faith, while at the same time very real about their struggles. Many of the guys who come participate in our parish's weekly hours of Eucharistic Adoration. Every Friday, following the 12:05 p.m. weekday Mass, a consecrated host is placed in a display called a monstrance. The monstrance is then placed on the main altar in the church. For the next twenty-one hours, people come into the church for a "holy hour," an hour spent quietly in the presence of Jesus in the Eucharist.

I had been to Adoration a few times during my conversion, but never for an hour and never as part of anything organized. As I was working my way through my ad hoc RCIA experience with Fr. Chris, he encouraged me to spend time each week in the chapel at another local parish that had 24/7 Adoration. I went a few times and it was always peaceful. I had often wondered what it would be like to make that a more regular thing, but I felt I was way too busy for that.

I thought, *Can't I just pray anywhere? I get the theology behind receiving Jesus' body and blood in the Eucharist, but do I really need to sit in front of it? What am I supposed to do there?* I think most converts can relate to these thoughts. There's nothing in Protestant churches like Eucharistic Adoration. Every once in a while in my old church there would be some people who would spend some time in the sanctuary praying, but it was pretty rare. After all, there's nothing special about a church sanctuary, in and of itself. If the atmosphere helps you focus on God, that's great, but there's really no objective difference from one building to another. For Catholics, obviously this isn't the case. While indeed there's nothing special about a building itself, the minute there is a consecrated host present, we are on holy ground. This is where the idea of Eucharistic Adoration comes from. In your first year in the Church, you need to get involved with this.

As the list made its way to me, I noticed there were time slots that went all the way through the night. "We really need some help during the two to five a.m. slots," Gary said. Gary was one of the guys in the group who always had two things going on: a smile on his face and a flyer in his hand. Gary is a pretty graceful guy, so when I saw that he was a little troubled by the lack of participation by some of us, I felt a little guilty that I hadn't signed up.

Friday nights? There's no way I can do that, I told myself.

Often during our busy season, we would have Saturday photoshoots starting at 8:00 a.m. We would work nonstop until 9:00 p.m. That's after doing two or three shoots on Friday. I am a total wimp when it comes to sleep. If I don't get enough I turn into a baby.

"OK, I'll take two to three a.m.," I said. I am also a recovering people pleaser.

When I told Estelle what I had signed up for she said, "That's great, honey. Just be quiet when you leave and come home. I need my sleep." She probably thought it was something I would do once or twice and then quit. I had wanted her to come with me but I knew that was probably not going to happen. Estelle had been doing better at Mass. She was no longer crying every week and she was really starting to put some things together in terms of what was happening in the Mass. This was leading us into some very interesting conversations about worship and faith. My wife is a powerhouse of a woman. She is very smart and also very insightful. She was beginning to see for herself some of the things I was so drawn to in Catholicism. The perspective she came from was much different than mine. Estelle was raised Catholic, but it never meant anything to her because it wasn't really a part of her life. She attended Catholic school all the way until her high school graduation, and she would tell you she never really felt close to God through any of it. Her faith came alive outside the Catholic Church, so imagine how strange it was for her to return more than twenty years, three kids, and one idiot husband later. There would be things said or done in the Mass that would make her visibly cringe. It's almost as if she had a mild form of ecclesial PTSD. Yet here she was. Standing (and kneeling . . . and sitting . . . and standing . . .) beside her crazy husband who had once told her Catholicism was nothing more than a superstitious religion that makes people try to earn their salvation. I had nothing but appreciation for her and the way she supported me in all this. Even though I wanted her to come with me to Adoration, I wasn't going to push it.

The first night I went, I showed up almost twenty minutes early. I didn't know whether to go to sleep and try to wake up at 1:20 a.m. or to stay awake until it was time to go. I went to sleep and woke up fast, fearing I would sleep through it. I ran out of the house and flew to the church. Normally it takes twenty minutes to get to church from my house. What I hadn't accounted for was the fact that in the middle of the night there is no traffic. I got there in ten minutes.

When I arrived, I was surprised to see about a dozen people in the sanctuary. On paper, there were three people assigned to each one-hour slot. What I would later learn is that often people who aren't assigned show up. There was even one elderly woman there, who I have been told often spends the entire night in the church. There were people spread throughout the sanctuary and everyone was completely silent. There were people in front of the altar on their knees and even one man lying on the floor. Others sat in pews and a few people walked around, evidently praying the Stations of the Cross. It was like nothing I'd ever seen before. *This isn't even some special event or holiday, it's just Friday*, I thought.

What had I just discovered? I didn't understand everything about what was going on, but I knew that this was a level of worship and devotion I had never encountered before. I knelt before the monstrance and stared at the host. "Jesus, I believe you are really here," I said under my breath. I made the sign of the cross and then found a seat.

No one had told me what you're actually supposed to do during Adoration. Are there certain prayers? Is kneeling the entire time required, or can you sit? I looked around a bit to see what everyone else was doing for clues. What I quickly discovered was that there didn't seem to be any prescribed activity. Some people were reading. Others were praying the Rosary, and still others just staring at Jesus.

I honestly had no idea what I would do to fill the entire hour. I couldn't remember the last time I spent an uninterrupted hour in prayer. I decided to begin with a Rosary. I remembered Fr. Chris saying that an incredible amount of grace is received when you pray a Rosary during Adoration. Instantly I felt the presence of God in an intense but peaceful way. After my Rosary was complete, I prayed for each member of my family, one by one. Then for certain people in my life who I knew needed prayer. My mom passed on February 7, 2018, and as a Catholic I now recognized that my prayers for her didn't need to stop. We were all devastated by my mom's death. The only thing that gave me any consolation was knowing that she was with the Lord. Ryan had died as well and I grieved for him immensely. I lifted his soul to God and asked for God to receive him into his mercy.

As a Protestant, I was always taught that prayers for the dead were useless. After all, once someone dies, their eternal destiny is sealed. I don't pretend to understand how God works all of that out, but what I do understand is that the Jewish/Christian practice of praying for the dead is a lot older than any Protestant objection to it. This has brought me great comfort and has been a source of healing for me in my grief. I never leave a holy hour without lifting up prayers for my mother, Ryan, and others who have passed.

As I continued, I thanked God for what he was doing in my life. I asked him to bless our business so that our needs would be met. Finally I asked God for one specific favor: "Please reach Estelle's heart and bring her here." I wanted her to join me in Adoration someday.

Before I was finished praying, Tom from the Tuesday morning group was walking in and smiling at everyone (it was OK to smile and wave as long as you didn't make noise). I thought, *He must be early*. I looked down at my watch. It was 2:59 a.m. The hour had flown by in what seemed like fifteen minutes. I drove home, crawled back into bed, and managed to fall back to sleep for about twenty minutes before I needed to get up and get ready for a photoshoot.

I hadn't expected to think about my weekly Adoration time other than as a duty to be fulfilled. However, I found myself throughout the week looking forward to the peaceful time with Jesus. Most people don't have a lot of peace in their day-to-day lives. There's always some kind of noise around us. For me, those weekly times spent in the quiet church with Jesus were becoming a new part of my growing faith. I looked forward to it immensely.

After a couple of months, I made the decision to switch my time from 2:00 to 3:00 a.m. to 10:00 to 11:00 p.m., due to more photography jobs starting earlier. The 2:00 to 3:00 a.m. slot had some pretty reliable guys, so I knew it would be covered. Even though it wasn't the same feeling as waking up in the middle of the night, I still cherish my holy hour.

Our anniversary that year was on a Friday. We decided to celebrate by taking a day trip in our 2004 Mustang Convertible. We had no idea where we were going, but we did have to check the forecast to make sure no rain would hit us (the top leaks). The Weather app showed clear skies to the west, so we hit the road and made our way across Iowa's back roads. It was already turning into a great day. We stopped at a town named Iowa Falls, where we had subpar pizza in a historic restaurant built inside an old theater. After that, we followed the GPS in Estelle's phone to a place called Eagle City Winery. It's literally in the middle of nowhere. We drove on gravel roads several miles before we made it. Our cross-country trek was well worth it. The place didn't look like much at first, but the people were knowledgeable and friendly. We picked a bottle of their specialty, black currant wine, and headed outside to share it under a modest shelter. Our conversation revolved a lot around our current situation.

Estelle always wants to know how I am feeling about things. She is rarely satisfied with one-word answers (which is great, because I rarely give them). We talked and talked about how we were living in this new reality. It was scary in some respects, but it was also very exciting. The best part about all of it was that we were truly in this together.

Our business was keeping us busy, but we always wondered if there was something more for us to do in terms of ministry. One of the toughest things for pastors who convert is the loss of identity. When a person serves in full-time ministry, it's not just a job, it's a calling. Leaving that behind to become a Catholic (and in my case a full-time photographer), leaves a person with many questions.

"Is God done with me?" "Will I ever preach again?" "What am I supposed to do with my gifts and desire for ministry?"

These questions get answered for different people in different ways. Some people become deacons. Some guys write books and go on speaking tours. Some guys teach in seminaries or Catholic schools. *What about me? What was I supposed to do?*

Estelle is not just my wife but also my biggest fan. She thinks I am a great preacher and was convinced that the moment I came into the Church, all sorts of opportunities would present themselves to me. After all, many of our Catholic friends for years had said things to me like, "The Church really needs guys like you!" and "If you became Catholic, you could do a lot of good."

I certainly didn't expect anything crazy to happen. After all, there are many people who are way smarter and way better than I am who have converted. It's not like I'm an anomaly. I'm just . . . well . . . *me!*

Estelle, on the other hand, was struggling with this. It had been almost a full year since I had walked away from my job and nothing seemed to be happening. The Pope hadn't called. The guys at the Coming Home Network were great to talk to (Marcus Grodi even sent me an autographed copy of one of his novels. It was great!). But contrary to what some people think, they don't just hand converts bags of money and well-paying speaking engagements.

I did get the chance to give a talk about my conversion at Greg and Sandi's church the previous December. It was an amazing experience that was well received. I had felt so alive that night sharing about my journey and love for my new Catholic faith. People responded very favorably and I was given an overly generous honorarium. We had hoped that this type of thing would become more regular, but at the time I hadn't received any other invitations.

"Maybe I'm just done," I told her. "Nobody needs another conversion story. No one needs another book about some guy realizing that the Catholic Church is the fullness of the faith. Maybe I'm just supposed to be a normal person who works a regular job and goes to church. Would that be the end of the world?"

"No way," she said. "This *can't* be it. There has to be more for you to do. You're too good!"

"No way," I said.

"Well, you're just wrong and I know," she confidently said. Man, I have a great wife!

After we talked out some of our fears and worries about our future, the conversation turned to how Estelle was feeling about being Catholic again. I had noticed she seemed to be doing better. She told me how she was growing more and more in her appreciation of our new church. She was picking up on more things that were making sense to her in a new way. We both remarked how biblical and Christ-centered the Mass is. She was feeling the power of worshipping God in such a different way than ever before. It was great hearing her excitement about what she was experiencing. It had been a long time since I had seen her like this.

We also talked about what we hoped would be different for us as we began another year of marriage. How could we experience less stress and more peace? How could we slow down? I considered bringing up Adoration again, and suggest that she start going with me, but I didn't want to push. She would get there when she was ready.

After some time had passed, we decided to head south along with our new favorite wine and pop in on our old friends Mike and Jen, who lived in Ankeny. We all slammed some Casey's Pizza (it's an Iowa thing), hung out for a bit, and then Estelle and I made our way back east on Interstate 80. "I have to be back by ten o'clock for Adoration," I reminded her (I am so subtle). It was getting late and we were running low on gas. I feared that by the time I dropped Estelle off at the house and turned around to head down to the church, I would be late. "Do you think we can make it?" I asked her. "Hey, why don't I just go with you tonight?" "Great idea," I said. My prayers had been answered. Now I just hoped she would like it.

I have never asked Estelle to go back with me. She just does. In fact, when I have been out of town on Friday's, she goes without me. We both have experienced the peace that weekly Eucharistic Adoration brings. I know for a fact it has brought us closer to God and closer to each other. We don't say much to each other about what we do during Adoration. She does her thing and I do mine. The fruits of it in our lives have been tremendous. We have often talked about how Adoration is like a spiritual reset button. After the craziness of daily life, having a standing appointment with Jesus is pretty incredible.

You need to do this. Find a place nearby that has weekly Adoration and go. Build it into your life instead of looking at your schedule every week and trying to make it fit. Make a standing appointment. Make it a priority. You can do it. It's only an hour. Use that time to pray for a deeper level of grace. Work through a devotional book; pour your heart out to Jesus. Make sure to allow time where you just sit there and let God speak to you. Trust me, he will!!

"Know also that you will probably gain more by praying fifteen minutes before the Blessed Sacrament than by all the other spiritual exercises of the day."—St. Alphonsus Liguori

Fast on Fridays

Why Friday? Christians have been fasting on Fridays, in one form or another, since the very beginning of the Church. Friday is significant because it was the day of Jesus' Passion. We are called by the Church to make every Friday a day of some form of penance. This not only unites our sufferings to the sufferings of Christ, but it's a Church-wide workday for our departed brothers and sisters in Purgatory who need our help. So what's it all about and why should you make this part of your first year in the Church?

Fasting is the practice of denying yourself something for the purpose of spiritual devotion. How does it work? You deny yourself something that you normally enjoy (such as food, entertainment, alcohol, etc.) for a set amount of time. There are lots of different ways to fast. The most common, in the Church, is to abstain from normal food for most of the day. There are varying degrees of practice when it comes to fasting. Some people will eat nothing but bread from midnight to midnight. Others allow themselves one normal meal at the end of the day. The idea is that you give up something so you can experience the sensation of denying yourself. It doesn't work if it doesn't hurt. If you're a vegetarian, it doesn't count if you don't eat meat. If you don't drink alcohol, then fasting from wine isn't a sacrifice. Remember, it's not so much about what you fast from, as it is about denying yourself something you really want. How does not eating, or watching TV, or whatever you choose to fast from, impact your spiritual life? It's actually not that complicated. When you fast, a few things happen that can help you grow in your faith immensely.

Denying yourself things that your body desires shows your body that its desires aren't the boss of you.

There's a fancy theological word for this idea, "mortification". Mortification is the process of "putting to death the deeds of the body" (Romans 8:13). We all know that our fleshly desires can get us into a heap of trouble. While not all fleshly desires are sinful, when we are ruled by any of them, the door to the abuse of our flesh swings wide open. Think about it. Most of our sin comes not from a desire for an evil thing, but rather from the perversion of a good thing. Our desire for our daily bread can turn into gluttony. The desire for sexual intimacy with our spouse can turn into lust. The desire for safety and security can turn into obsession and control. The desire for the resources we need to provide for our family can turn into greed. Fighting the battle against our fleshly desires is a lifelong struggle that often leads to a cycle of sin, guilt, shame, and frustration. Fasting helps us battle against these desires by bringing the flesh under submission to the Spirit. Remember Jesus' words, *"The spirit indeed is willing but the flesh is weak" (Matthew 26:40)*. Listen to how the Apostle Paul describes the battle: *"I punish my body and enslave it" (1 Corinthians 9:27)*; *"Live by the Spirit, I say, and do not gratify the desires of the flesh" (Galatians 5:16)*. This doesn't mean that we should all starve ourselves to the point of physical danger, but what it does mean is that we need to show our flesh who is boss. We need to train ourselves in the practice of self-denial. As we do that, our resolve against temptation grows, as does our ability, with God's grace, to stand against it. Think of fasting as spiritual weight lifting. Much in the same way we train our physical bodies through painful but beneficial exercise, we need to train our spirit as well. No pain, no gain.

Fasting is a form of penance that satisfies some temporal punishment of our sin.

Temporal punishment is the consequence of our unhealthy attachments to things of the flesh. When we are forgiven our sins through the sacrament of Penance, the eternal punishment is absolved, but the temporal punishment of the damage sin has done to our souls must still be dealt with. That's because we still live in these weak bodies that have not yet been glorified. St. John reminds us that *"what we will be has not yet been revealed" (1 John 3:2)*. The damage that sin has caused our soul is restored when we do penance because it demonstrates our love of God is greater than our love of sin. Because fasting is a form of penance, it can repair the damage.

Fasting is a form of penance that can satisfy some temporal punishment of *other's* sins.

In the *Catechism* there is a section that speaks about the Communion of Saints. The basic idea is that, as the body of Christ, we are all intimately connected because of our common baptism and faith in Jesus. Death does not break this connection. The saints in Heaven intercede for the saints on Earth. Many of the great saints of the Church fasted more than any of us would ever try. That should mean something to us. In all of this, we must remember Jesus' words about fasting. *"And whenever you fast, do not look dismal, like the hypocrites, for they disfigure their faces so as to show others that they are fasting. Truly I tell you, they have received their reward."* *(Matthew 6:16)*. Don't post on social media about your fast. Don't make it public knowledge. Don't brag about it. In fact, if at all possible, keep it to yourself. If you get this wrong, your fasting could actually be hurting you instead of helping you. If you need people to notice how holy you are because you are fasting, then congratulations—you just completely defeated the entire purpose. This doesn't mean you can't talk about it with anyone. Maybe you are fasting with others because that helps you stay accountable. That's fine. It's when you go out of your way to parade your fasting to people out of pride that it becomes a problem.

Notice that Jesus didn't say *if* you fast, he said *whenever* you fast. This shows us that for Jesus, fasting wasn't something reserved just for the super-spiritual Christians. Fasting was and is something that has been a regular practice of Christian devotion. In your first year in the Church, it should be yours as well. Fasting is not easy, nor is it fun, but I think at some point you will realize it is making you stronger in the war against sin.

What You Need to Not Do

Don't overcommit.

As a new Catholic, it's easy to see all the devotional practices you never knew about and feel like you want to tackle them all. It's exciting to learn about the resources the Church offers the world and jump right into a ton of stuff. You'll hear stories of how this particular novena or consecration changed someone's life. You'll read things about the practices of great saints and think to yourself, "I need to do that!" You may even have some people at your new church challenge you to join them in a certain fast or retreat. Try to avoid the trap of over commitment. If you take on more than you can handle, you might be setting yourself up for failure. Don't let yourself feel the pressure of living up to what other people do. You need to prayerfully and practically figure out what will work for you. Jesus said that a person who first sets out to build without counting the cost is foolish. Count the cost of what you choose to do with the new resources you find in the Church. You don't want to wind up feeling like a total failure because you weren't able to do everything that everyone else does. Start with things that are easier and work up from there. You'll get there!

Don't undercommit.

It would be crazy to join the Catholic Church and not partake in any of its devotional practices. The Church has so much to offer you. Don't waste your opportunity by being unwilling to change or grow. There's a whole world out there for you to discover. You joined the Church for a reason. Incorporating these new practices into your life will help you grow in your relationship with Jesus and his Church. Start with the things mentioned in the previous section and work from there.

Don't announce to the world your new devotional practices.

If you haven't read the Sermon on the Mount in a while (Matthew 5–7), I suggest you take a look at it. Jesus has a lot to say about practicing your "righteous deeds" for other people to see, and none of it is good. It's a normal thing to talk about things you're excited about. There's nothing wrong with discussing these things with people close to you, but avoid the temptation to post your devotional practices on social media. Rather than impressing people with what you do devotionally, let them instead be impressed with how full of joy you are. Let the world see the fruit of your devotional life rather than the practices themselves. Remember, Jesus never condemned the practices done by the Pharisees, but he certainly condemned their need to be seen by other people. God is your audience and judge. He sees it all and that's what matters.

Books

As a new convert to the Catholic faith, you probably have had a book or two given to you by some well-meaning Catholics, or maybe even some scared Protestants. I remember when a pastor friend of mine told me to read a certain anti-Catholic book in the hopes that it would wake me out of my craziness. We had been meeting together occasionally to discuss my journey. He was concerned I was making a big mistake and wanted to help me come to my senses. The book he gave me to read didn't help his cause. It actually confirmed what I was feeling. It offered nothing new, and basically rehashed many of the arguments against Catholicism I had already overcome. I felt bad for him, but I had to tell him that it didn't work. We haven't met since.

I don't know if you're a reader, but when you became a Catholic you opened yourself up to a treasure of books. It's true that you don't need to be a Catholic to read and enjoy books about theology written by Catholic masters like St. Thomas Aquinas or St. Augustine. However, as a Catholic, they will mean much more to you now. I'm not suggesting that every new convert tackle St. Thomas Aquinas's Summa Theologica or St. Augustine's Confessions right away, but it's pretty amazing to think about these great works of theology and philosophy as part of your new family library. People are always writing new books (thanks for reading this one), but there's something to be said for reading old ones. Many of the great written works of the Catholic Church are far older than most of the Protestant denominations that exist today. Just because something is old doesn't mean that it's true or valuable, but when it comes to the works of the Christian faith that have stood the test of time, nothing can hold a candle to written works of the saints (and other respected Catholic authors).

As a convert, I would recommend you start to open yourself up to some of these works. I know it can be a daunting idea to try to read books like *The Summa*, but there are plenty of others that aren't as intimidating. I once found a giant old book at a consignment store called <u>The True Church of Christ</u>. It has tons of artwork, articles, and indexes. My favorite chapter is called "The Shortest Way to Settle Disputes." That chapter is seventy pages!

Here's a list of some popular books that were written by saints or other well-respected Catholics. Some are hundreds of years old. Some are more recent.

1. *The Story of a Soul* by St. Therese of Lisieux
2. *Interior Castle* by St. Teresa of Avila
3. *Finding God's Will for You* by St. Francis de Sales
4. *True Devotion to Mary: With Preparation for Total Consecration* by St. Louis de Montfort
5. *The Imitation of Christ* by Thomas à Kempis*
6. *Orthodoxy* by G. K. Chesterton*
7. *The Faith of Our Fathers* by James Cardinal Gibbons
8. *Signs of Life: 40 Catholic Customs and Their Biblical Roots* by Scott Hahn
9. *Butler's Lives of the Saints* (concise edition) by Michael Walsh
10. *Upon This Rock* by Stephen K. Ray

All of these books are great and may prove useful to you. There are countless others that also may serve you. Much of what you need to read depends on where your interests lie and where you need encouragement. I often found myself drawn back to *The Faith of our Fathers* because it's such a great defense of Catholicism. Even though I had converted, I realized that I would still need to have the chops to handle tough conversations with friends who didn't understand things like purgatory or the papacy. For me, this book proved the most helpful. When I really wanted to understand what it meant to honor the Blessed Virgin Mary, St. Louis de Montfort's work was something I turned to. For you, it may be something completely different. The point is, find what works for you and start exploring.

Of all the books written, as a convert there are two you absolutely need. They are *The Catechism of the Catholic Church* and the Bible. ALL OF IT!

The *Catechism* stands apart from the list because it's the official explanation of the Catholic faith. It explains in very accessible language and style what the Church believes and teaches about virtually everything you need to know. The *Catechism* is an absolutely essential book for all Catholics, but especially for new converts. Think of it as a basic guidebook for Catholic belief and application. I can't tell you how awesome it is to have a written, official statement of belief. Whatever questions you have about your newfound faith, the *Catechism* probably has the answer. If you don't have a copy, get one immediately.

Secondly, if you haven't done so already, you need to get yourself a new (or should I say old?) Bible. I have many Bibles. I have the ESV (English Standard Version) Study Bible (the cool, young, hipster reformed theologians like this one); I have the NIV (New International Version) Life Application (this was the one that all my friends at Calvary Chapel used even though Pastor Joe preached from the King James); and I still have the old RSV (Revised Standard Version), which I received when I was in third grade at the United Methodist Church. I have a Bible called <u>Da Jesus Book</u> that a friend brought back from Hawaii. It's sort of in English. I have so many Bibles, but when it was time to convert, I knew I needed a version that contained *all* of the books.

It's crazy that for the vast majority of my life as a "Bible-believing Christian," none of the Bibles I had contained all of the books that belong in the Bible. The modern Protestant versions of the Bible contain only sixty-six books, while the Catholic versions contain seventy-three. These "extra" seven books comprise what is known in the Protestant world as the Apocrypha. Catholics do not refer to those books as the Apocrypha because the word literally means "doubtful or false." Catholics grant these books the same status as the rest of the books of the Bible. So if you look for a section in your Catholic Bible called the Apocrypha, you won't find it. As a convert, this was troubling. When I was a Protestant, I had believed that the Catholics added these books to the Bible at the Council of Trent in the sixteenth century. They did so to combat Martin Luther's attacks against the evil doctrines of purgatory and more specifically the selling of indulgences. The book of Maccabees supports the idea of offering prayers for the dead, which Luther opposed because it ultimately leads to the doctrines surrounding purgatory. According to what I had always been told, the Catholics tried to pull a fast one on the world by coming out with a new list that included these books for the first time. The Reformers held fast to the original Bible, and that's why the Protestant versions do not include those books (or if they do, they list them under a separate section). This is all, of course, hogwash. At one point in my arguing against Catholicism, I remember telling Devin, "If you can produce an authoritative list that contains the Apocrypha before the Council of Trent, I will become a Catholic immediately." I don't remember his exact response at the time, but once I did a little digging what I discovered shocked me.

The Synod of Rome was held in 382 (which is significantly before the sixteenth century) and delivered to the world the first official list of books that were actually considered Scripture. That list includes all of the books that comprise the Catholic Bible. It was the Reformers who removed books from the Bible. In fact, Martin Luther also wanted to remove books from the New Testament. Hebrews, James, Jude, and Revelation were all books Luther had issues with. His followers talked him out of it, but he was able to convince them to get rid of these seven books from the Old Testament. I know there are plenty of Protestant scholars who will still argue for the exclusion of these books, but for me and the vast majority of Christians, it's pretty clear which version of the Bible is accurate.

Once that discovery is made, it's time to make sure you have all the Scripture God gave to the world through the Church. Get yourself a new Bible and get reading! You have some catching up to do! Reading the Bible as a Catholic, for me, is a whole new experience. Certain passages take on new meaning and everything seems to fit better when read through the lens of the teaching of the Church. I know you will have this experience too. Read your Bible now more than ever. The Bible is God's gift to you given through the Church. Because you now belong to the Church, you can actually understand what it means! Gone are the days when you have to create your own interpretations or embark on a wild-goose chase for the true doctrine or interpretation. You are not on your own when it comes to figuring out what it all means. With the Bible in one hand and the *Catechism* in the other, you can rest assured that the Holy Spirit is indeed "guiding you into all truth" (John 16:13).

Brethren

"Therefore, since we are surrounded by so great a cloud of witnesses, let us also lay aside every weight and the sin that clings so closely, and let us run with perseverance the race that is set before us,"
(Hebrews 12:1).

"When he had taken the scroll, the four living creatures and the twenty-four elders fell before the Lamb, each holding a harp and golden bowls full of incense, which are the prayers of the saints."
(Revelation 5:8).

"And the smoke of the incense, with the prayers of the saints, rose before God from the hand of the angel."
(Revelation 8:4).

The flyer on the bulletin board promised more than 180 relics would be on display in the church basement. I was intrigued. A relic is something physical that is associated with a saint. Most of the time, it is either a piece of bone, hair, or clothing. These items date back centuries, even to the apostles themselves. They would be on display at our local parish for one night only. Estelle and I thought this could, at the very least, be interesting to our sons, so we invited them to come with us on the promise that they would see some "really cool old stuff." I was a little put off by the unadvertised ninety-minute presentation given by the priest who brought the relics. It's not that anything he said was bad, I just hadn't prepared my sons (and one of their atheist friends), for the long talk before seeing the relics. I sat there praying that this guy would wrap it up so we could get to the good stuff. It was all fine for me, but I knew my ability to bring my boys to "Catholic stuff" was fading. They waited patiently until the presentation was over and then we (and three hundred others) headed downstairs to see the relics. It was pretty amazing to see them and read about all these Christians I knew nothing about. As a convert, you have to come to understand that you are part of the largest, longest-lasting organization on the planet. The saints are your spiritual ancestors, but they are also your brothers and sisters. This is something you've never experienced before and it's incredible. It's doubtful that beyond learning about the apostles, and perhaps some basic information about whoever founded your particular denomination, you have ever spent much time learning about the saints. It's true that some saints have become popular even outside the Catholic Church, but typically not for the right reasons. We know that St. Patrick was from Ireland and we think he liked the color green. Do we know anything about his spiritual life or what he did for the Church? We know that St. Nicholas dressed up in red and gave people presents (did he really?), but are these legends even accurate? At the end of the day, what does it all have to do with Jesus?

Years ago a Catholic woman described to me how whenever she lost something, St. Anthony would help her find it. Back then I thought that was ridiculous. When Estelle and I needed to sell our home, we were encouraged to bury a statue of St. Joseph in the front yard. Seriously? There are some strange beliefs and practices out there when it comes to the relationships Catholics have with the saints. How does all of this fit into your faith as a convert? What does it all mean?

Like everything else, there are people who take things too far. Don't let that scare you off. The saints are real and according to Scripture they play an important role in our lives. I know as Protestants we were taught that this was ridiculous, but like everything else we've learned, when you look at what Scripture says and what the Church teaches, you see this is reality. The book of Revelation describes heavenly worship complete with the saints offering their prayers to God. What need could they have for prayers in Heaven? The answer is, they pray for us! Just as we pray for each other here on earth and for the souls in purgatory, the saints in Heaven pray for us. We are all connected. We are all the family of God. Death does not change that. Think of when Jesus took Peter, James, and John up the mountain of Transfiguration (Matthew 17:1–8). Who did they see? Moses and Elijah! Were they dead? Were they alive? How can you describe that other than as a window into a greater reality than we can possibly understand here on Earth? I like the way St. John put it when he wrote:

> *"Beloved, we are God's children now; what we will be has not yet been revealed. What we do know is this: when he is revealed, we will be like him, for we will see him as he is."*
>
> *(1 John 3:2).*

When Jesus was transfigured on the mountain, Peter, James, and John caught a glimpse of that reality and it included this amazing connection with those brothers who have passed from death into life. They are, as the Scripture says in Hebrews, "a great cloud of witnesses." Think about what that means. Consider how amazing it is that those great men and women who have gone before us into the throne room of God Almighty are there interceding for you. What does this mean for you practically? It means that you can ask for their intercession. You can look to the saints as your inspiration, not only in what they have accomplished while they lived on Earth, but also as a powerful intercessor as they now worship Jesus in his presence. The book of James says, *"The prayer of the righteous is powerful and effective" (James 5:16)*. The Church teaches that those prayers do not stop just because a person's body has died.

You could spend your entire life learning about the saints and not even scratch the surface of who they are and what they have done. One of the things we were encouraged to do at the relic presentation was to seek out a saint that would be special to us. Then we should learn as much about him or her as we could. Finally, we should ask for their intercession. I had chosen St. Ignatius of Antioch. During your conversion, you receive the sacrament of confirmation. In this sacrament, you choose the name of a saint that you want to especially help you in your life and faith. St. Ignatius was the bishop of Antioch and was installed in his position by the Apostle Peter himself. Ignatius had done something to offend the Roman emperor Trajan, most likely refusing to compromise his faith in Jesus Christ. Ignatius was sentenced to die in Rome by being devoured by lions in the Colosseum. On the journey to Rome, Ignatius wrote letters to the Christians in seven cities. In these letters, he declares that he is ready to die for his Lord. He even goes so far as to forbid anyone from trying to prevent his death. He considered himself an offering to God and wanted nothing more than to die a martyr. He got his wish in AD 108.

When I read about this man, my heart was moved. How much of my life have I spent trying to find the easy way? Let's face it; in our American society it's easy to be a Christian. Nobody is going to come and kill you. Nobody is going to take your property. The worst thing most of us will ever suffer for our faith is being made fun of, or rejected. I know these are trying times for many Christians across the world, but here in the United States, we are so spoiled. I often wonder how Christians today in America would react to the type of persecution the early saints suffered. I would like to say I would allow myself to be eaten by lions for the faith, but honestly, it was a struggle for me just to quit my job and become Catholic. Learning about the saints and praying for their intercession not only inspires me to a greater level of holiness, it also opens the door to many great graces. In your first year in the Church, I want to encourage you to pick at least one saint that you will learn as much as possible about. Ask that saint for his or her intercession and help in your life and faith. Never forget that you are not alone. You are a part of something amazing that transcends not only culture, language, and worship style, but even the veil between Heaven and Earth. We all praise God together in the Mass, and we all walk through this life together.

Roman Catholicism is like a tool box filled with everything needed to build a great palace. All of these tools are meant to help people enrich their faith and increase their devotion to God. Jesus is a master carpenter. He knows how to build things. He knows how to create. He created this universe. He created life. He created everything that was created! His ultimate creations are his saints. His desire is that you and I would join them. The saints have been given no more gifts than you and I. The sacraments, Scripture, prayers, devotions, the great cloud of witnesses, the Mass; all of these things are the tools that God has created and given to us as gifts. These gifts are powerful and effective. If we use them, we will grow stronger in our love for Jesus and in the grace that he offers. In your first year in the Church, you are like a little kid opening dad's tool box for the first time. Take them out and use them. Master them. Get to work. Build your life on the solid rock of the word of God, using the tools that God has given you. His promise to you is that if you seek Him, you will find Him. If you hunger and thirst for righteousness, you will be satisfied. Jesus' Church has the best tools ever created for spiritual growth. And now you have access to all of them. Isn't this Catholic stuff awesome?!?!?!?

Chapter 9

The Mary Stuff

For many converts, nothing is harder to incorporate into your faith than the Mary Stuff. Across the spectrum of Protestant churches, you will find at least something that resembles Catholic teaching on almost every aspect of the faith, except the Mary Stuff. You can find sacraments, Scripture, liturgy, prayer, the belief in apostolic authority, the saints, and even the adherence to the ancient creeds of the Church. But for some reason, when it comes to the Mary Stuff, the Protestant churches shut it down immediately. For most of my life, I thought the Roman Catholic beliefs about Mary were nuts. Some of my hang-ups were the result of misunderstanding. I didn't always recognize the difference between asking for intercession versus worship. The statues were an issue as well. I knew the Bible forbade the worship of idols and whenever I saw Catholics bow down in front of statues, it made my skin crawl. When I was considering conversion to Catholicism, I had to do so in spite of some of the things about Marian devotion that freaked me out. The songs, the prayers, the tattoos, the apparitions, the decals on the backs of low-riders. Some of this stuff was scary, and some of it was just plain goofy. Was I really going to become one of those guys? Did I have to buy into all of the Mary Stuff to become Catholic?

I was meeting with a friend whose mother had recently converted to Catholicism. He did not approve of her decision at all. In fact, it really bothered him. He told me that despite her conversion, she wasn't caught up in the "bad stuff" most Catholics believe. She didn't pray the Rosary or have any statues or images of Mary. "She's the most Protestant Catholic I know," he said. I remember thinking how strange that was, but in a certain way it made sense. Why couldn't Catholics just decide what they wanted to do and not do when it comes to the Mary Stuff? I knew that belief in the doctrines of the Immaculate Conception, Mary's Perpetual Virginity, and the Assumption were required, but do all Catholics have to do the other stuff?

Maybe you've had similar thoughts. Maybe you've felt the awkwardness that comes when you make the transition from having almost nothing to do with the Mary Stuff to suddenly finding yourself surrounded by statues, rosaries, and Salve Reginas. How should you handle this? What if it makes you feel uncomfortable? How will you process such a drastic change? It's almost as if you've been adopted into a new family, and you aren't sure what to call your new mother. It feels weird to jump into her lap the first day you meet and tell her what you want for Christmas. At the same time, you see how much all your new brothers and sisters love her. You feel like you may be missing out on something, but you don't want to pretend to have the same relationship with her on your first day that they have enjoyed their entire lives. I can completely understand these feelings. I certainly have been there. My first year in the Church started with uncertainty and apprehension when it came to the Mary Stuff. As the year progressed, things changed dramatically for me. I still don't have any statues in my front yard or decals on my Harley, but I am so blessed to call Mary "Blessed Mother."

What You Need to Know

The Advent season in 2016 was a rough one for me. My mom was in the middle of her struggle with pancreatic cancer. She was fighting hard, but the cancer was growing and complications were mounting. We were doing all we could to make the most of the time we had together, but it was so painful watching my mom's body deteriorate. She prayed and prayed for a miracle, but everything seemed stacked against her. It felt like my whole world was being shaken. I have a very close relationship with my parents and the thought of losing my mom was devastating.

In the middle of all this, I was growing more and more convinced that I needed to become a Catholic, but I was totally afraid to quit my job. I was in what many converts have referred to as "no-man's-land." That's the place you occupy when you have become convinced of the truth of Catholicism, but you haven't decided you can convert. It's a tough spot. I bet you know what I mean. I had shared my struggle with our senior pastor, Mike. He was both my boss and my friend. He shared many of my struggles about what was happening in our denomination. We would often commiserate together about the chaos around us, but the thought of leaving to become a Catholic was something he wouldn't ever consider. When I told him what I was thinking, his reaction led me to believe he thought this was just something crazy Keith would work through. He didn't say much. Maybe I just needed time. Maybe I just needed to find something to get excited about in my church. We started talking through ideas for our upcoming Advent sermon series and, as we often did, we divided the weeks between each other.

The week of December 5, it was my turn to preach. The sermon series title we chose was "Who Gets the News?" It dealt with the different instances in Scripture when people were given the news that Jesus was coming. The first week we tackled Zechariah. He was the father of John the Baptist. When Zechariah heard the news from the angel Gabriel himself, he didn't believe and was struck mute as a punishment.

It was my turn to preach and the next person in line to highlight was . . . you guessed it, Mary. As I dug into that week's sermon prep, I began to notice something strange happening to me. I found myself reacting to the texts about Mary *emotionally* in a way I had never experienced before. I had done plenty of Bible study on Mary. In fact, when I was in college, I wrote a research paper on all the Catholic doctrines about the Virgin Mary. I did a detailed study on every verse that mentioned her in Scripture (what Protestant does that?!?). What happened to me as I prepared that sermon was like nothing I'd ever experienced in all my years writing sermons. Every time I would sit down to write, I would be overcome with emotion. This kind of thing just did not happen to me. *What was going on?* I wondered. I considered the fact that I was in a lot of pain due to my mother's illness. Maybe that was why I was being emotionally triggered. Or maybe there was more.

That Sunday, I preached a sermon called "Mary Gets the News" to seven hundred or so United Methodists. I told them how she must have been more amazing than we could ever imagine for the angel Gabriel to greet her the way her did, "Hail, full of grace!" I contrasted the greeting he gave to Zechariah (who was called "blameless"), and wondered what was so special about this young woman, who at the time had done nothing remarkable (or so I thought). Next, I unpacked the prophecies about Mary in the Old Testament, starting with Genesis 3:15. I explained the ancient Church Fathers' view that Mary was both the "New Eve" and the "New Ark of the Covenant." I also related how she was the "Woman" referred to in Revelation 12, "clothed with the Sun." It was like I just opened every Catholic apologetics book I'd ever seen and started dumping it on these unsuspecting Methodists. I was on fire. I felt so filled with the Holy Spirit as I delivered that sermon. I hadn't stopped to consider if it would offend anyone. As the thought of that came to me, I noticed people in the congregation with tears in their eyes. Something was happening not just to me, but to them too. After the sermon, there were even a few people who came up to the communion rail and knelt down with tears in their eyes in prayer. It was amazing. More than a few people came to me that week and said they felt something powerful that morning. I had never seen a reaction to a sermon like that before, let alone one about the Blessed Virgin Mary. I wasn't sure how to process what was happening, but one thing I knew was there was more to the Mary Stuff than I was ready for.

For me, what started as an intellectual exercise (writing a sermon), turned into what seemed more like a relationship. I had not expected that. Was it all a figment of my imagination or was I tapping into a previously undiscovered (to me) treasure of the historic Christian faith? Like so many other things, when a Protestant converts to Catholicism, it's as if a new world opens.

In reality, it's the old world. The stuff of Catholicism (and especially the Mary Stuff) is far older and more widely celebrated than any of us ever thought. This is crucial information for converts. Here's what you need to know:

- The Roman Catholic doctrines concerning the role of Mary are rooted in Scripture.
- Marian devotion dates back to the earliest writings of the Church Fathers.
- There are some things you must believe as a Catholic, but other things you may choose to believe or not.
- Proper devotion to the Blessed Virgin Mary will actually increase your love and devotion to Jesus.

> *"If then we are establishing sound devotion to our Blessed Lady, it is only in order to establish devotion to our Lord more perfectly, by providing a smooth but certain way of reaching Jesus Christ."*
>
> St. Louis De Montfort

> *"We never give more honors to Jesus than when we honor his Mother, and we honor her simply and solely to honor Him all the more perfectly. We go to her only as a way leading to the goal we seek— Jesus, her Son."*
>
> St. Louis de Montfort,
> True Devotion to Mary

What You Need to Do

Go at your own pace.

The Mary Stuff is powerful. In your first year in the Church you need to approach it like an expensive bottle of fine wine. When I drink wine, it's usually from a bottle that costs less than twenty dollars. It all tastes about the same to me. A few weeks ago, a friend took me to dinner. He's a wine snob. He knows what good wine is all about. He ordered a bottle that I am sure cost more than my entree. I wondered, *How much better could it be than the cheap stuff I usually drink?* My friend was so excited about this wine. When the server brought the bottle, he smelled it, swished it around, and then tasted it. It easily met his approval and we were ready to drink. As soon as it hit my lips, I got it. The texture was like silk. The taste was far and above anything I'd ever had before. I marveled at what I had been missing my whole life (since I turned twenty-one, of course). It was very good, but I made the mistake of not pacing myself. Rather than drink it in slowly and savor every nuance, I carelessly downed it. I wasn't drunk, but later that evening I felt its effects. It was way too much, way too fast. I look forward to trying it again at a more reasonable pace. When you're used to a cheap version of something, the real thing can be overwhelming. The Mary Stuff is like that. As Protestants, we had a cheap version of the understanding of the Blessed Virgin Mary. We viewed her as a woman who just happened to be chosen to give birth to Jesus. There was nothing remarkable about her (other than her obedience in that moment). She was understood to be a sinner like the rest of us. She lived a relatively normal life. She had a husband and kids. She died and that was it. She was close to Jesus, but not more than anyone else at that time. We "honored" her in songs and Christmas carols, but once Advent was over, we didn't give her much attention. Cheap wine.

As we came into Catholicism, we began to experience something completely different. We began to see her through the lens of the entire Bible. We came to understand what the Church (even up through most of the Reformers) all across the world have believed, taught, and experienced since the beginning. We have tasted the deep, rich, and powerful understandings about the Blessed Virgin Mary and we are amazed. If we move slowly, we can savor every hint of flavor and texture. We can feel the difference in so many ways. Fine wine.

Study Scripture that refers to the doctrines about Mary.

Most of the hang-ups converts usually have about the Mary Stuff come from the mistaken idea that the Catholic doctrines about Mary are unbiblical. The reason for this is because as Protestants we didn't have much of a choice. First, we were taught that there must be explicit chapter and verse proof texts for everything Christians must believe. Second, we were taught that the verses about the Mary Stuff *can't* mean what the Catholics say they mean. Why? Because that would make the Catholic point of view biblical (and we can't possibly have that).

When Catholics defend their beliefs about Mary from Scripture, it's often rebutted with an argument about interpretation, or lack of clarity. What's ironic to me is that many of the verses in Scripture that support the Catholic doctrines give a greater weight to the entirety of Scripture, and not simply a few proof texts here and there. Many of the Catholic positions aren't arrived at because a verse explicitly says, "Mary was protected by God from the stain of original sin by a special act of grace so that she could be the pure vessel for the Incarnation." The Catholic Church doesn't treat the Bible that way. Catholic doctrines aren't based solely on a proof text. Remember, the doctrines existed in one form or another *before* the New Testament was even assembled. If every Christian doctrine had to first be proven from Scripture, then the first Christians would have had no basis for anything. I know this is a different perspective than we converts are used to, but hang with me here. The Bible itself tells us that not everything Jesus taught was explicitly written down immediately (or ever) as Scripture (John 21:25). Not even everything the apostles taught was written down. St. Paul writes to the Thessalonians,

> *"So then, brothers and sisters, stand firm and hold*
> *fast to the traditions that you were taught by us,*
> *either by word of mouth or by our letter."*
> *(2 Thessalonians 2:15).*

Think about that verse. It's stating the obvious truth that eludes so many people. The apostles passed down the faith to the Christians through what they wrote and what they said. Therefore, it's of vital importance to test everything taught, not by whether or not there is an explicit verse, but rather, whether the idea is part of the overall teaching of Jesus and his apostles? This is where the notion of Sacred Tradition comes into play. Sacred Tradition refers to the entirety of the teaching of the Church, not just what's been written down in Scripture. This is not to say that there are new and innovative doctrines added to the faith over the years. Let this sink in: everything the Catholic Church declares today as official dogma (a doctrine that must be believed) has always been present in the Church. Ideas have been developed and unpacked over the course of history, but there has never been a moment when anyone said, "Here's this new revelation that contradicts something we believed before." Understand, this doesn't apply to practices and disciplines of the Church, which may be changed and modified (for example, saying Mass in vernacular languages, required fast days, clerical celibacy). This only applies to those specific beliefs that are recognized as divinely revealed by God for all time and all people.

Even though this may seem like an exclusively Catholic understanding of the relationship between doctrine and Scripture, it's really not. Protestants do it too. They don't like to admit it, but some of the doctrines that Protestants believe are not explicitly taught in the Bible. For example, there is no chapter and verse that says "God is a Trinity." Yet the doctrine of the Trinity is understood by most Protestants to be absolutely necessary for Christians. I don't disagree, but how did they arrive at that conclusion? The answer is that they accept what the Church has always taught about the nature of God. The doctrine of the Trinity is implicitly taught in Scripture, and it is also taught by the early Church Fathers. This view was expressed in the early Church Councils of Nicaea (325), Constantinople (381), and many others. When Protestants profess their belief in this doctrine, they do so in a way that pays homage to both Sacred Scripture and Sacred Tradition. The same is not true of the Marian doctrines. For some reason, the rules change when it comes to the Virgin Mary. As a convert, you don't necessarily need to embark on a comprehensive study of all the Marian doctrines and their origins. However, it's helpful to know that they all have their roots in Scripture. This will help you as you incorporate the Mary Stuff into your faith. Here's an example to help get you started:

The Immaculate Conception

In the year 1854, Pope Pius IX wrote a document called *Ineffabilis Deus*, in which he infallibly declared: "The Most Blessed Virgin Mary was, from the first moment of her conception, by a singular grace and privilege of almighty God and by virtue of the merits of Jesus Christ, Savior of the human race, preserved immune from all stain of original sin."

Where is this idea found in Scripture? Take a look.

> **Luke 1:28:** Mary is declared by the angel Gabriel to be "full of grace."
> **Luke 1:42:** Mary is "blessed among women."
> **Luke 1:46–49:** Mary is called "blessed" because of the great things God has done in her.
> **Genesis 3:15:** Mary is the "woman" whose seed will crush the head of the serpent.
> **Luke 1–2; Samuel 6:** Mary is the new Ark of the Covenant.

Theologians and several Church Fathers have made two biblical observations about Mary that apply to her Immaculate Conception. They both deal with analogies about Mary taught in Scripture. This is a little different way to read the Bible than some of us converts are used to, but it is certainly not new to Christianity. In fact, Jesus himself used this technique all the time to declare truth and to help people understand his teaching. Jesus referred to himself as "the Good Shepherd," "the Gate," "the Bridegroom," and others. John the Baptist declared Jesus was "the Lamb of God." The fact that these were analogies in no way meant they weren't true (when Jesus referred to himself as "the Living Bread," it was both an analogy and literally true at the same time). In our everyday language an analogy is basically saying "this is *like* that," but in the language of the Bible, often analogies carry a heavier implication. More like "this *fulfills* that," or "this is the *better version* of that." Think about it, Jesus isn't just *like* a door; he in fact is the perfect and only way to the Father. Jesus isn't *like* a sacrificial lamb; he actually was the fulfillment of everything lambs were sacrificed for. Jesus isn't *like* bread; he himself tells us, "for my flesh is true food and my blood is true drink." (John 6:55). In the Bible, things can be both analogies and literally true at the same time in a deeper way. In fancy biblical study language, this is referred to as "typology." Think of typology as an enhanced analogy carrying a deeper level of meaning.

This understanding of biblical analogies/typologies with regards to Mary is what led the Church to these doctrines about her Immaculate Conception. When you start to see this, it will blow your mind.

The first analogy/typology is Mary as the "New Eve". This was discovered by first- and second-century Church Fathers like St. Justin Martyr, St. Irenaeus (yeah, it's that old), and up through the Middle Ages by men like St. Thomas Aquinas. What these saints observed as they studied Scripture were some interesting parallels between Eve and Mary. The first mother of humankind was Eve. Eve was created without the stain of original sin, but sadly fell to temptation in the Garden of Eden, along with Adam.

Whereas Mary, by her obedience, became the new mother of all the faithful (John 19:26–27). Scripture refers to Jesus as the "New Adam" (Romans 5:12–18) and by his obedience purchased life for those who were dead in Adam's sin.

In Genesis 3:15, there is a prophesy about a "woman" whose seed would crush the head of the serpent. Everyone understands the seed of the woman is Jesus. Everyone also understands the serpent is Satan. Therefore, the Church teaches that the "woman" is rightly understood to be Mary. She is the New Eve. Eve was conceived (or created) without original sin. Mary is "blessed" (or "more blessed") among women, including Eve. Therefore the Church recognizes that she too, by God's grace, was conceived without the stain of original sin. So basically, Jesus is the New Adam and Mary is the New Eve. The first Adam and Eve were born without original sin, yet were disobedient, which led to death for all mankind. The second "Adam" and "Eve" were also born without original sin, but were obedient, which led to life for all mankind.

The second analogy/typology the Church Fathers saw in the Scripture dealt with Mary as the new "Ark of the Covenant." The Ark of the Covenant was the box that contained the remains of the stones on which God wrote the Ten Commandments, Aaron's (Moses' brother) rod that budded (look that up), and a golden pot containing manna (bread). The Ark was understood to be the holiest item on Earth. It contained the physical presence of the word of God. It was so holy that if anyone on Earth even touched it (other than the priests, or those of the family of Kohath, who had to use special poles to move it), they would die (2 Samuel 6:1–7).

The Ark of the Covenant was special because of what it contained. That doesn't mean that the Ark was just a normal box. It was built to exact specifications given by God Himself to Moses. The Ark was covered in gold and made to be approached and handled with extreme reverence.

Early Church Fathers like St. Athanasius, Gregory of Thaumaturgus, and St. Ambrose made the connection between the Ark of the Covenant and Mary. In fact, if you read Scripture closely, there are some amazing parallels between what happens when the Ark is brought back to Jerusalem after being captured, and Mary's visitation to her cousin Elizabeth in Luke 1. There are volumes written about these parallels, but I'll share a couple of examples here:

> *"And David was afraid of the Lord that day; and he said, "How can the ark of the LORD come to me?"*
> *(2 Samuel 6:9)*.*

> *"And why is this granted me, that the mother of my Lord should come to me"*
> *(Luke 1:43)*.*

> *"As the ark of the LORD came into the city of David, Michal, the daughter of Saul looked out of the window and saw King David leaping and dancing before the LORD..."*
> *(2 Samuel 6:16)*.*

> *"For behold, when the voice of your greeting came to my ears, the child in my womb leaped for joy"*
> *(Luke 1:44)*.*

The same word for "leap" is used in both instances. The idea is that when David encounters the Ark containing the presence of God, he "leaps" for joy in the same way Luke tells us the unborn John the Baptist "leaps" for joy when the new Ark of the Covenant (Mary) comes to him.

Here's another interesting parallel. In Exodus 40, Moses is told by God to set up a tabernacle (place of worship) and to put the Ark inside. A cloud of the "glory of the LORD" overshadows the Ark. In a similar manner, Gabriel tells Mary she will be "overshadowed" by the Holy Spirit as she conceives Jesus (Luke 1: 34).

Are these parallels found in Luke mere coincidence? Or is Luke trying to show us something? I know this is a different way to proof-text beliefs from Scripture than most converts are used to. We are accustomed to chapter-and-verse snippets that support a belief we already have. However, this is not the only way (and often not the best way) to study Scripture and understand doctrine. It's certainly not the way the earliest Christians developed the faith. Remember, when your litmus test for Christian belief is the chapter-and-verse proof-text method, you can run into serious trouble. This is one reason why there are so many opposing Protestant theologies and viewpoints. If all it takes to form a view on any given subject is to find a chapter and verse proof text, then virtually anything and everything can be argued, and it often is.

As you encounter doctrines about Mary (and other things), understand that for Catholics, it's not so much about proof-texting as it is about understanding the nature of God's revelation through both Sacred Scripture and Sacred Tradition. The two are linked together in a way that provides a greater understanding than could be achieved if not for the other. The Marian doctrines have their roots in Scripture, but the meaning is not always clear until we are guided by the Church. Think of how much we all missed before we converted! Aren't you thankful that God has called you home into the fullness of the faith, into His holy Church?

One final text that has helped me tremendously as I have come into the Church is Revelation 12: 1–2. Right after describing a vision of the temple (and the Ark) in Heaven, St. John writes, *"A great portent appeared in heaven: a woman clothed with the sun, with the moon under her feet, and on her head a crown of twelve stars.* [2] *She was pregnant and was crying out in birth pangs, in the agony of giving birth."*

I know there are many who interpret this woman to be symbolic of the nation of Israel, but it also certainly applies to the Virgin Mary, Queen of Heaven. For me, this has been helpful, because I have come to understand that Mary's prominence was given to her by God. If He saw fit to crown her in Heaven, then who am I to deny her importance and allegiance? How many other people have been seen clothed in the sun and crowned in Heaven? How many others have been called "full of grace" by the angel Gabriel who stands in the presence of God (Luke 1:19)? How many others have been called the "Mother of my Lord"?

If God cared enough about a wooden box to require that it be wrapped in pure gold to house his Word on tablets, then how much more would he wrap the vessel who would carry the incarnate "Word made flesh" (John 1:14) in purity? About how many others did Jesus say to his Disciple, "Behold your Mother"? The doctrines about Mary are more biblical than any of us ever knew.

Begin to learn about approved Marian apparitions and miracles.

I mentioned at the beginning that the idea to write this book came to me while I was on a trip to Bosnia-Herzegovina in 2018. This had been my second trip to the village called Medjugorje. Medjugorje is a place where six children have claimed to have seen and heard from the Blessed Mother in a series of apparitions. An apparition is a supernatural vision in which a person actually physically sees and/or hears a message from the Virgin Mary. This vision may or may not be seen by others around them, but they are convinced it is real. Marian apparitions have been reported since the fourth century in one form or another, but it's only in the last few hundred years that this phenomenon has become prevalent. A quick web search will reveal dozens of reported claims of Marian apparitions, but the Church has only formally recognized a small number. There are three types of Marian apparitions when it comes to the Church. There are those that are approved, those that are disapproved, and those about which the Church has not issued a formal decree. Medjugorje has not been approved at this time (it is still under investigation), but that doesn't stop millions of pilgrims from going there. In my brief time there, I have experienced an incredible sense of the presence of God. I have seen a few things that could be considered "miraculous" (weeping statues, strange things appearing in photographs), but I never heard or saw the Virgin Mary, or saw anyone healed of a disease, but others I know personally make claims like that. Some people think Medjugorje is of the devil, but I can't imagine how the devil would want so many people worshipping Jesus, going to confession, and committing themselves to prayer and fasting. I'm not here to convince anyone about Medjugorje (that's not my job), but I can tell you this much, as a convert, learning about some of the historical, public miracles that have occurred in Church-approved places like Lourdes, France, Fatima, Portugal, and Guadalupe, Mexico, will blow your mind. Just because the Church has approved an apparition doesn't mean that a person is required to believe it; it simply means that it has been found to be "worthy of belief." You can choose to believe or not. However, if you take a look at the evidence, I think you will be amazed. I'll start you off on the journey with two of the biggies:

Guadalupe, Mexico

"Our Lady of Guadalupe" is the title given to the woman seen in the visions of St. Juan Diego in 1531. Juan was walking along the base of a hill on the morning of December 9, when he saw a supernatural vision of a young woman. She identified herself as the "Virgin Mary, Mother of the very true deity." She asked Juan to have a church built on the site of the vision. Juan reported the visions to his bishop, who asked him for a sign. Juan saw her again and she insisted that the church be built. Juan spoke to the bishop again, who told him to return to the site of the first vision and ask for a miraculous sign. That same day he saw her again and she told him that on December 11 she would indeed give him the sign. Unfortunately, on December 11, Juan's uncle was very sick, so Juan decided to stay with him rather than go see the Virgin Mary (his uncle must have been quite the guy!). The next day, Juan's uncle was near death, so Juan set out to find a priest to administer last rites. Juan was afraid to see the vision again (since he stood her up), so he took a different route. Unfortunately for Juan, Mary wasn't stuck in one place. She appeared to him and gently scolded him for missing their appointment. "Am I not here, I who am your Mother," she said to him. She then told him his uncle would be fine and that he should return to the hill where she first appeared to him. She instructed him to gather some flowers from the top of the hill and take them to the bishop as proof that she was real. In December, the top of the hill was normally barren, but Juan found a bunch of Castilian roses, which weren't even native to Mexico. He gathered a pile of them in his tilma (a long piece of fabric) and took them to the bishop. When he approached the bishop, he unfolded the tilma and the roses fell out. Everyone there was shocked to see that on the tilma was an incredibly beautiful large image of the woman. This image is known throughout the world as the image of Our Lady of Guadalupe.

The next day Juan found that his uncle was cured, just as the Virgin had said. This miraculous image on Juan's tilma is an undeniable miracle. It has been scientifically studied numerous times, and the results have led to more questions than answers. The fact that the tilma still exists is in itself a miracle. The tilma was made from cactus fibers that normally last just a few years. The tilma has been on display for nearly five hundred years. The image has also been subjected to numerous scientific tests and no one can explain its origin from a natural point of view. It has no sketch under the pigment. The pigment itself was declared by biochemist Richard Kuhn in 1936 to be of unknown origin. Not to mention there have been many new discoveries within the image that have baffled those trying to explain it as merely a painting. The eyes contain tiny reflections of fourteen people (many say Juan Diego and the rest of the witnesses) who weren't seen until the image was studied under magnification of 2500X. Skeptics, of course, will argue that this image was the work of a sixteenth-century Indian painter. I've also read that some people even deny that Juan Diego was a real person. However, the majority of the evidence lends itself to the conclusion that something truly miraculous took place in 1531.

Fatima, Portugal

In the spring of 1917, three shepherd children encountered an apparition of the Virgin Mary. They were herding sheep near their home when they saw what they described as a "Lady more brilliant than the sun." She gave them messages and secrets. She even foretold that two of the three children would be taken to Heaven soon (they both died within three years) but that the girl named Lucia would live a longer life so she could spread the message (she died at age 97). Their claims were of course met with skepticism, but the children insisted the events were real. The Virgin promised the children that she would give a miraculous sign, "so that all may believe." The Virgin even gave the date and place where the sign would occur. It didn't take long before the word got out (some newspapers even printed it), and on October 13, 1917, roughly seventy thousand people gathered at the promised place, called Cova da Iria. According to reports and eyewitnesses, it had been raining heavily. The ground and all the people were soaked. Photos taken on that day show people standing in mud. Eyewitnesses described the events, which can only be called miraculous. The heavy rain stopped, the clouds parted, and the sun appeared more dim than normal. Then the sun began to "dance" and zigzag in the sky. It also emitted multicolored light. At one point, it appeared as if it were heading toward the earth, frightening the onlookers. Just before it would crash to the earth it returned to its normal place in the sky. The miracle lasted around ten minutes. After it was over, the people and the ground that had all been soaked by the heavy rain were inexplicably dry. This is not some legend from thousands of years ago. This happened one hundred years ago. There are photographs. This event made headlines in secular newspapers. There were tens of thousands of eyewitnesses.

Why should a convert care about stuff like this in their first year in the Church? I don't know if these miraculous events about Mary interest you or not. Not all Catholics care about Marian apparitions, but for us converts, the idea that miraculous events are occurring that validate what the Church teaches about Mary and her role in the faith is at the very least interesting. It may even change your life. As I mentioned earlier, my friend Greg's life was turned upside down during a visit to Medjugorje. He is one of thousands who have experienced a deep conversion as the result of this phenomenon. Does that prove that the apparitions there (or anywhere else) are true? The answer to that question depends on who you are. No one can make anybody believe something they don't want to believe, but if you are the least bit open to the idea that the Virgin Mary has been trying to reach the world with her messages of devotion to her son, then perhaps there could be something there for you.

Pray the Rosary.

The Rosary is a great way to put a proper devotion to Mary into practice. The mysteries draw us into the life of Christ. We acknowledge and worship who God is in the Glory Be, we pray the prayer Jesus taught us in the Our Father, we ask the Blessed Mother for her intercession and we acknowledge who we are when we say, "Pray for us, *sinners*."

The great thing about the Rosary for converts is its simplicity and its repetition. It's easy enough that you can learn it quickly, and structured enough that you don't get lost or overwhelmed. It takes a little getting used to, but if you commit yourself to praying a daily Rosary, you will be amazed at how your devotion to Mary will help you draw nearer to Jesus.

What You Need to Not Do

Don't worry about what other people do.

Let's be real. To converts, some Catholics can appear wacko when it comes to the Mary Stuff. At times, I have found myself a little uncomfortable when I have let other people's devotion freak me out. I have a growing devotion to the Blessed Mother, but I don't have giant statues in my house of Mary just yet. Maybe someday I'll get there, but for me I still struggle with the way I have seen some Catholics treat an image of the Blessed Mother with more reverence than the Holy Eucharist. I'm not here to judge anyone else (you shouldn't either), but when you first enter Catholicism, some of the Protestant objections to the Mary Stuff can hang on. I think it's absolutely important to completely agree with everything the Church teaches about the Blessed Mother, but if watching people bow before statues and endlessly focus on Mary (and not her son) makes you squirm, don't worry about it. Just move on. People handle different things in different ways when it comes to their faith. That's OK. Don't judge them for where they are, and don't feel like you have to do the same things in order to be Catholic. Just be real about where you are, and see where it takes you.

Don't ignore her.

If you've struggled with the Mary Stuff before entering the Church, you may feel a desire to put her on the back burner. That's a mistake. As a Catholic, you believe that Mary is the best intercessor there is. Why would you not want her to intercede for you? As a Catholic, you also believe that Mary is your spiritual mother. When Jesus gave Mary to John at the foot of the cross, he did not say, "Take care of my Mother." He said, "Behold, your Mother" (John 19:27)*. This is understood in a certain sense for John who took her into his home, but also in an ultimate sense for all the Church. Jesus gave His Mother to all of us. She has now become, in a very real sense, the Queen Mother of the kingdom. You can read about the role of the Queen Mother in the Old Testament. For example, in 1 Kings 2, Bathsheba (the mother of King Solomon) is given a place of prominence in the kingdom. This was the custom in all of the kingdoms. It was not the wife of the king who had the privileged position, but rather the king's mother. If Jesus is rightly understood to be the ultimate king in the Davidic Kingdom, then it's rightly understood that Jesus' Mother would be the Queen. This understanding is confirmed when we see the previously mentioned glorified vision of Mary in Revelation 12.

> ¹"A great portent appeared in heaven: a woman clothed with the sun, with the moon under her feet, and on her head a crown of twelve stars. ²She was pregnant and was crying out in birth pangs, in the agony of giving birth."
>
> (Revelation 12:1–2).

As I've said before, it's pretty hard to deny that this is a vision about the Blessed Virgin Mary. She is crowned the Queen of Heaven and Earth. She is our mother. Why wouldn't you want her intercession? She is a treasure and help to all of us. You will discover this the more you look to her. The more you pray the Rosary and meditate on her life, the more this will make sense. You may not be ready to tattoo the Tilma from Guadalupe on your forearm, but do not make the mistake of ignoring the Blessed Virgin Mary.

Don't worship her.

Human beings are great at taking good things and making them ultimate things. We often take the good things God gives us and turn them into idols (sports teams, musicians, political figures, etc.). We are so prone to look to creation rather than the Creator for our salvation and significance. This can happen even with the Blessed Virgin Mary. As a convert, praying to anyone other than Jesus is something that can be tricky. As Protestants, we all believed that prayer and worship were synonymous. The notion that anyone other than Jesus could even hear our prayer was not part of our faith. As Catholics, we now understand that the saints can and do hear our prayers and intercede for us. Because the Blessed Virgin Mary's role in our faith had been ignored for so long, there can be a desire to swing far the other way, into dangerous territory. Mary leads us to Jesus. Her job was and is to bring God into the world, and now she exists to bring the world to God. As long as we remember to keep her role in the proper perspective, we will experience an amazing level of spiritual growth. However, we must remember that Mary is a creature. She was created by God. She is not all-powerful, all-knowing and all-present. Those are attributes of God alone. We can look to her for her intercession and inspiration, but not for salvation in the same sense as we can with her son. He is our Lord and yet she brings Him to us, and brings us to Him. Worship God alone! This is the best way to honor Mary.

Devotion to Mary ultimately is about Jesus. This is something you will come to understand the more time you spend in the Church. For someone to be devoted to Mary, they must truly adore and worship Jesus. Otherwise, they have forsaken Mary's role and even her strongest desire. This goes for all the saints. They are all a means to an end. They exist to help us become closer to Jesus and to grow in holiness. No true saint (especially Mary), would desire for themselves the worship that rightly belongs to God alone. Where the saints are now (Heaven), they know more and more the fullness of the glory of God. They surround us with help and intercession as we journey toward Jesus. We can offer our devotion to them, which will enhance our love for Jesus, not detract from it.

Chapter 10

Catholicism and Culture
"Who do men say that I am . . . supposed to be?"

We all have a desire to fit in. No matter where we go, we take our cues about what's acceptable in any given situation by looking around and seeing what other people are doing. The last thing most of us ever want is to feel out of place. If we go to an event where people are dressed up, we want to be dressed up. If we attend a gathering where people are dressed casually, we don't want to be that guy who wears a suit and tie. We all feel sorry for that guy! When it comes to church, most people are even more conscious about blending into the crowd. Church is usually a place where you don't want the focus on yourself. So how do you "fit in" in Catholicism? Is it just about what you wear or how you look? Is it about what you drive? Should we all run out and buy fifteen-passenger vans? If only it were that easy!

Churches are well known for being places where appearances matter. Some of us grew up in churches where we had to dress up to fit in. We had our "church clothes" on every Sunday to show that we understood the importance of . . . wearing church clothes. Others came from churches where the style was more laid back. If you wore a suit and tie to a church where everyone dressed in street clothes, you would reveal to everyone that you were completely clueless.

Fitting in, in church is not just about what you wear. It's about understanding and participating in the regular practices and culture of the church. That involves much more than clothing. In church, culture is the combination of many things, including how people interact with each other, and how they incorporate the faith in their everyday lives. Culture can dictate certain taboos as well. These are things that are viewed as "un-Christian" by the group as a whole for a variety of reasons. Often times "fitting in" is as much about what you don't do, as it is about what you do.

For example, growing up, I had a strong belief that drinking alcohol was generally sinful and not something Christians did. My parents drank wine with their dinner, or to relax, but I never saw either of them drunk, so I didn't think that was a big deal. However, in my view, beer and hard liquor were absolutely un-Christian. It's strange how we arrive at certain ideas about sin not from Scripture alone (even as Protestants), but more from what we are taught and from what is culturally regarded as Christian or secular. Especially in the Evangelical/youth ministry world of the late twentieth century, there were certain things that for Christians were off limits, while other things were deemed acceptable. Maybe you experienced this. Much of my faith upbringing was influenced by a wide variety of Protestant perspectives ranging from the ultra-fundamentalism of some of the youth groups I attended, to the mainline denominationalism of my parents. I also watched a lot of Christian television, listened to a lot of Christian radio, and listened to a ton of Christian music. It was clear that in addition to believing what the Bible says about Jesus, there were certain rules that governed the lives of Christians. The problem was these rules didn't always line up with the Bible, or even each other. For example, according to some people, Halloween was Satanic, but it was OK if you dressed like a Bible character. All secular music was bad, but certain bands like U2 were OK (even though they never claimed to be a Christian band). R-rated movies were strictly forbidden (except *The Passion of the Christ*). And drinking alcoholic beverages under any circumstances was just about the worst thing anybody could ever do (even though Jesus turned water into wine).

When I started hanging out with Catholics, I quickly learned they had different rules. I was once invited to a Fish Fry at the Knights of Columbus. It was a Friday in Lent, and these legalistic Catholics didn't eat meat on Fridays because of some "man-made traditions," but when the priest came to the table with two pitchers of beer, I was speechless. *You won't eat a burger on a Friday, but you can have beer?* I thought. These Catholics were nuts!

During my first trip to Medjugorje, before we even boarded the plane, one of the other pilgrims, a guy named Butch, slammed his credit card on the airport bar and said to the entire group, "This round is on me!" The entire trip, people drank alcohol and had a great time. I never saw anyone drunk or even slightly out of control. In fact, everywhere we went it was normal to see people with a beer or glass of wine talking and laughing together as though it were no big deal at all. This was not the world I was used to.

When Estelle turned twenty-one, we went to lunch at Ruby Tuesday's in the mall. She wanted to order a Strawberry Daiquiri and talked me into ordering one for myself. We were horrified when the parents of one of my youth group kids came and sat in the booth behind us. I thought I was going to lose my job for sure. In hindsight, I'm sure they didn't think twice about it, but at the time I was convinced I had done something terrible. *I was the youth pastor, and there I was in the mall, drinking alcohol!!* Drinking alcohol (in moderation) is not condemned anywhere in the Bible, yet for some churches, it is completely taboo. The same could be said for using tobacco, dancing, or even watching movies. Part of fitting into a church involves understanding the core values of the group as a whole. That usually isn't discovered simply by reading the Bible.

Maybe your experience has been different, but I am sure of this: When you come into the Church, you find not just a different liturgy and hierarchy, but also a different culture. Catholic culture just feels different. And different Catholics have different cultures. Depending on where you came from, you may experience things that leave you wondering, "Where in the world am I?" The first time I went to the Mass where they do the "Blessing of the Throats," I had an experience like that. That was followed by viewing an "incorruptible body" of a saint who had been dead for eighteen hundred years. His body is in a glass case under the side altar of the church! You will have your own experiences of culture shock in your first year. It's OK. It's totally normal, just roll with it.

Another aspect of Catholicism that is interesting to point out is that across the world, and across the spectrum of humanity, Catholicism binds people together despite their cultural differences. In other words, the goal in Catholicism is not uniformity of culture, but rather uniformity of faith. This was not always the case for some of us converts. Some converts come from churches where the culture itself was almost indistinguishable from the faith. I'm not speaking necessarily about national-istic culture, as much as I am about societal culture—in other words, the cultural aspects that are defined by our own choices. This is especially true in the new age of Protestant church planting. New churches spring up all over the country planted by young, hip, culturally savvy pastors, who seek to redefine what a church should look like. For example, hipster churches, where everyone wears skinny jeans, flannels, scarves, and vintage-looking glasses. There are country western churches where, you guessed it, everyone dresses like a cowboy. There are prosperity-gospel churches, Pentecostal churches, and even what I call "Little House on the Prairie" churches (the women wear only long dresses like Laura Ingalls). There are mainline Protestant churches where everyone still wears nice clothes and sings hymns, and there are beach churches, where people wear flip-flops and flowered shirts. My point is that all of these defining characteristics are more *cultural* rather than *theological* (don't tell the hipsters I said that, they get very touchy about their reformed doctrine). In Catholicism, what may strike you is that church culture typically isn't defined in the same way. There still is a culture, but it's different. In Catholicism, there can certainly be an ethnic component present, but within ethnicities there is not the same segmentation according to worldly styles that defines the type of church a person attends.

Our identity as Catholics lies not in our cultural preferences (the type of clothing we wear, the music we listen to, the prod-ucts we buy, etc.), but rather in our participation in the liturgy and the Sacraments. The normal traits of whatever culture we find ourselves in will be present, but it is secondary to the culture created by our belief in the teachings of the Church. In other words, you can be white, black, Latin, Asian, Native

American, rich, poor, middle class, a Gen Xer, baby boomer, millennial, or any other generation. You can be a person who loves jazz, rock, hip-hop, country western, or even pop music. You can ride a Harley or a Kawasaki. You can be a Mac or a PC! You can wear skinny jeans and fake glasses, or you can wear a suit and tie. You can be a rugged outdoorsman, or a pencil-pushing accountant. You can be whoever you are. Catholic culture tends to lean more on what's going on *in* the church rather than what's going on *outside* of it. Many Protestant churches today are taking their cues about the type of culture they want to create from the world. In an attempt to reach the culture with the gospel, many Protestant churches try to make the culture of their churches look as much like the outside world as possible, while at the same time inserting the gospel into it. This is often referred to as "redeeming the culture." Redeeming the culture is about taking aspects of the culture and incorporating them into the church, but without any of the inherent sinfulness that may naturally accompany it. Sometimes this works and sometimes it doesn't. For example, musical styles can be adapted to create meaningful worship experiences that don't have to result in sinfulness. The same may not easily be said when the church tries to appeal to the progressive liberal cultural elements of society that are so closely connected to issues like abortion, marriage equality, or freedom of religion. When churches try to tell the progressive liberals of the world, "Hey, we are just like you," sometimes things get a little weird. What we have often seen in those situations is not that the church redeems the culture, but rather, the culture compromises the integrity of the church. This has long been the case in the mainline Protestant denominations like the Presbyterian Church USA, the ELCA, the Disciples of

Christ, and my old stomping grounds, the United Methodist Church. These churches once stood as relatively orthodox institutions that at the very least would claim Scripture as their final authority. Those days are long gone. Most of these groups have been so ravaged by compromise that they barely resemble what they once were. What starts as a cultural olive branch ("come to our church, we are just like you"), often devolves into a complete dismantling of any call to repentance and holiness ("why *should* we come to your church when you're just like us anyway?"). All of these denominations have experienced huge losses in membership in the last fifty years.

This culture-church collision isn't confined to liberalism. Some conservative churches have seen their attempts at redeeming the culture go a little haywire as well. Some of the most baffling displays of this occur in churches where financial and worldly positions are regarded as indicators of God's favor. Pastors and Bible-teachers make the big bucks, live in mansions, drive expensive cars, and wear expensive suits, all to show that they are approved of by God. The promise to the congregation is that they too can become rich if they will give generously and be as faithful as their leaders. As you can imagine, scandal and abuse of power often accompany these situations. When the desires of the flesh are overly gratified, the Spirit is not in control. Sadly, bad things can and do occur as a result. People are abused and cheated. Manipulation and control become the dominant leadership style, and often sin creeps in at all levels. The cultural implications of churches like this tend to favor those who look the part and say the right things. There is no emphasis on "denying one's self" or "taking up your cross." Instead, the focus tends to be on what God can do for the people if they have enough faith. It just so happens that what "God can do" is always about more money, power, and possessions. Hardly the stuff of the gospel.

The world I came from was somewhere in the middle of that. We tried as hard as we could to maintain what we considered an orthodox theology. Our cultural compromise revolved more around catering to the lukewarm, nominal Christian whose faith in God (and church attendance) was subject to the typical demands of the modern child-centered lifestyle of North American middle-class Christianity. Many families would come to church when it was convenient for them, but the moment their child's sports season started, they would vanish for months. Our job at the church was to give them some nice messages that pointed them toward faith in Christ, but we had to tread lightly on the ramifications of the gospel's call to put Jesus first in everything. We wanted to see God move mightily (and sometimes we did!), but more often than not, I felt we gave people a false sense of security that they could have both the world and their soul. For us, redeeming the culture meant we had to cheer for kids at their games during the week, because we wouldn't see the families in church on Sunday. We had to let them know that they were fine just as they were, but at the same time try to call them to a greater level of Christian discipleship. That's a tough needle to thread. Pastor Mike is way better at it than I was.

There is nothing inherently wrong with the idea of redeeming the culture; it's just that the Catholic Church has a different approach. As a convert, I bet you have noticed it. In the Catholic Church, the way we redeem the culture starts with ignoring it. Think about what that means. The Catholic Church doesn't seek to be culturally savvy or "relevant" in terms of its liturgy, theology, or structure. The Catholic Church doesn't change with the times the way many other churches do. The result of this is that people can come to the Church without checking their cultural identities at the door. Additionally, the Catholic Church has understood, from the very beginning of its existence, that the way to redeem the culture is to change the hearts of the people in it. When people of the culture become people of God, whatever is happening in the culture will reflect that. That's exactly what happened in the early Church. The culture was dominated by paganism, death, and evil. The early Church stood against it and changed the world. This isn't to say the Church has always done this perfectly. There are certainly periods where worldly power and corruption made its way into the Church. But the promise of Jesus that "the gates of hell will not stand against it" has ensured that He is keeping things under control. The Church (like the nation of Israel) will have periods of greater obedience and blessing, and also periods of disobedience and punishment. God disciplines his children. None of this changes God's faithfulness. He keeps his promises. When the Church experiences dark times, we can rest assured that God will not abandon his flock. History has proven this to be true.

What does all this have to do with your first year in the church? A ton! Who you are as a Christian is not subject to the culture of your church anymore. You can be who you are. You are subject only to Christ and to His Church, and His Church doesn't change like shifting sand the way the culture does. The rules have changed for us converts. In some ways it will be easier (I can drink a Strawberry Daiquiri and not worry), and in some ways it will be harder (now we are obligated to go to church *every* Sunday!).

In all things, we have been given the freedom to worship and obey God without focusing on all these man-made rules anymore. We don't have to look around to see how everyone else dresses or talks. We don't have to pretend to be passionate about whatever the trendy cause of the day is. We don't have to keep up with the Joneses to prove that we are loved by God. We can simply come together with all people from all walks of life to celebrate a common liturgy and receive the same graces in the same sacraments.

So how do you fit into Catholicism? Be yourself. Follow the liturgy. Follow the teaching of the Church. That's all you need to worry about. Nobody cares about what you are wearing or how you talk. Nobody cares about what you drive. Nobody cares if you have a beer with your pizza or a cigar afterward. Love God. Work hard. Take care of your family. Be nice to others. Just be real. It will all be fine.

Chapter 11

Gaining Your Soul and Losing the World

The night I finally knew I was going to convert was a moment in time I will never forget. It was in the spring of 2017. I had been working through the material with Fr. Chris that would prepare me to enter the Church, but I was still wrestling with the decision. I knew this feeling. I had felt it many years before.

One night, during our yearly church camp, we were having a Communion service for the students. My good friend Mike was leading the service and at the moment when the bread and juice were brought out, something in me broke. This was during the time when Devin and I had been trying to convert each other, the late 1990s. All of the arguments and apologetics had me so tied up in knots, but I was too afraid to admit that I could be wrong. When it all hit me that night, I ran out of the lodge and called Devin. Through tears, I confessed to him that I was feeling the Lord's call to the Catholic Church. I braced for him to react in excitement and say something like, "Ha! I knew it!!!! Woo-hoo." Instead, he gently assured me that God wanted me home, and that everything would be OK. Unfortunately,

I didn't listen to his assurances. When I was faced with the reality of the sacrifices that would be required of me, I chose to put those feelings which were drawing me to the Catholic Church on the back burner. I was too afraid of the cost. That's a decision I have come to regret with a depth of remorse known only to me and those closest to me. In the years that followed, my life and faith suffered greatly. There were seasons when I thought God was through with me.

Years later, I found myself in nearly the exact same place. I was hearing the voice of God, but struggling with what obedience would mean for my family. I didn't care anymore about being right or winning an argument. Those days were long gone. When God shows a person the depth of their brokenness and restores them, many of the things in life that mattered most seem so foolish. All that mattered to me now was serving God, and loving my family well.

So in the spring of 2017, I was not only asking God to show me the truth, I was asking God to make a way for me to follow it. If he was calling me to convert, there had to be a plan, a way, something to make this possible. I had no idea what I was looking for, but I was sure that something would happen to open a door so that I could make this transition. "God, if you want me to become Catholic, make a way", was my prayer.

My normal daily routine is to wake up a little earlier than Estelle, make the coffee, and spend some time in prayer before starting the day's tasks. One morning as I was praying, I felt a strong sense from the Lord that I needed to connect with a guy named Steve Ray. Steve Ray is a former Baptist who converted to Catholicism and now makes documentary movies, gives talks about the Church, and writes books. I had seen a few of his talks on YouTube and was impressed by his knowledge and passion. I had never talked to him or seen him in person. *How and why could I connect with Steve Ray?* I thought. *What does that even mean?* I had the day off from work at church for some reason and had made plans to have an early supper with my friend Greg in Iowa City. When Greg walked into the restaurant and sat down, I was ready to tell him my "revelation" from God that morning about Steve Ray. I didn't know if Greg even knew who Steve Ray was. We had never discussed him before. We said hello and he raved to me about the burgers this place served. Before we could even order, Greg's phone went off. It was a text message from his wife Sandi: "Hey Greg, tell Keith that Catholic apologist and author Steve Ray is giving a talk in Silvis tonight. Maybe you guys should go."

"Have you ever heard of this guy?" Greg asked. I couldn't believe what he just said.

When I told Greg about my morning "revelation," he knew we had to make this happen. It was a good thing we decided to meet at 4:00 p.m. because Silvis is about an hour away from Iowa City. We snarfed our burgers and drove straight to Our Lady of Guadalupe parish.

When we arrived, Mass was under way. The church was packed. Even though I couldn't receive the Eucharist, I often went forward for a blessing. I wanted to get as close as I could to Jesus. After my blessing, I knelt down to pray. I stared up at the large wooden crucifix and began to pour out my heart to God. "God, what is happening to me? I believe you want me to become a Catholic, but I need you to make a way. There has to be a way! I can't just do this without any plan or ability to take care of my family. Jesus, I need you to make a way."

As clearly as I've ever felt God speak to me, from the cross, Jesus said, "I *am* the way. You don't need me to make a way, you just need *me.*"

That night Steve gave a great talk about how the early Christians suffered and died rather than compromise the gospel. These brave men and women gave up everything rather than deny the Faith. Who was I to put a condition on my obedience? Who was I to say to God, "I'll follow you, but only if you make it easy for me"? In essence, that's exactly what I was saying. In my entire quest for the true faith, I had finally come to the place where I was faced with the reality of what the gospel calls us to give up in order to attain the faith:

> *"If any man would come after me, let him deny himself, and take up his cross and follow me. For whoever would save his life will lose it, and whoever loses his life for my sake will find it"*
> *(Matthew 16: 24–25)*.

What I realized that night was, even if I lost my income and career, if I gained Jesus, it was more than worth it. Jesus calls us all to pick up our cross and follow him, but in order to truly do that we must deny ourselves. That can mean different things for different people. For me, it meant denying my need for security. My cross in that moment was not the loss of my life, but rather the loss of my control. Despite all that God had been showing me, I still wanted to be in control. I wanted to know that everything would be OK according to my plans. Jesus showed me that night that following him into his Church would require obedience and trust, without conditions. None of us truly need anything more than what we already possess in Jesus. Jesus is not a means to an end. He is the ultimate end.

After Steve's talk, Greg said to me, "We're going to talk to him. He has to meet you." I'm not normally the guy who goes up and talks to the speakers at events, but Greg wasn't giving me a choice. As we made our way past several older women waiting to show Steve pictures of their grandkids, Greg said to Steve, "This is Keith Nester. He is a Protestant pastor who is feeling called to become a Catholic. Can you please write down your cell phone number and give it to him?" (I love Greg). Steve looked at me and said, "Brother, I know exactly where you are. You need to either become Catholic right now, or once and for all turn away from it and never look back. If you don't, you'll go crazy." Then he gave me a copy of his book, *Upon This Rock*, and wrote his cell number on the inside cover.

On the way home, I told Greg, "This is it. I'm doing this. I have to." When I got home I told Estelle everything that had happened that night. She hugged me tightly and said, "Keith, I am so proud of you. Whatever happens we are going to be all right." After that there was no turning back.

* * *

I joined the Catholic Church on October 8, 2017. Greg, Sandi, and my friends Yvonne and Verlyn from my old Methodist church in Davenport (who also converted) came for the Mass. When I stood to receive the Eucharist for the first time, I was so humbled. I had finally done it. I felt fulfilled and at peace. Not long after, when it was time to pass the peace, I felt a tap on my shoulder. I turned around and none other than Steve Ray himself was standing there. "Welcome home, brother. You'll never look back." He was right.

I don't know what it has cost you to join the Catholic Church. Perhaps you don't even know either. Strained relationships, the loss of the familiar, and a career perhaps? Maybe none of those things apply to you. Maybe for you joining the Catholic Church was more about leaving your old life of sin behind and turning to a relationship with Jesus for the first time. Not everyone who converts to Catholicism comes from another church. Some converts come straight from the world. What has it cost you? Independence? Control? The ability to do whatever your flesh desires? Whatever the cost is, it's worth it.

> *"The kingdom of Heaven is like a treasure hidden in a field, which a man found and covered; then in his joy he goes and sells all he has and buys that field"*
> *(Matthew 13:44)*.*

Think about this: Everything the man owned had to be sold in order to purchase that field, but that wasn't the end of the story. It's only the beginning. The real work begins once the field belongs to the man. Buried treasure is rarely just below the surface. It's often buried down deep in the ground, requiring the one who finds it to be willing to sweat and suffer to get it. The desire to find it is fueled by the anticipation of the reward of achieving something amazing. If the treasure were nothing special or remarkable, the man would surely give up. However, in this parable, Jesus says that the man is so full of joy because this is no ordinary treasure. This treasure is the kingdom of God.

As a convert, we are a lot like this man. God has shown us

where his treasure is buried. He has shown us all that is present in his Church. For so long it has been hidden from our eyes. With joy we purchased the field. We gave up what we needed to. Now we just need to dig. Your first year in the Church, you will do a lot of digging. You will get messy. You will get blisters. You will sweat. You will grow tired. Others may look at you and say, "What are you doing down there?" Don't worry. Keep digging. The kingdom of God in its fullness has been given to you. Jesus has called you into it. It's all worth it. The promised reward far surpasses anything you could imagine. As St. Paul wrote, "But, as it is written,

> *"What no eye has seen, nor ear heard, nor the human heart conceived, what God has prepared for those who love him"*
>
> *(1 Corinthians 2:9).*

That verse isn't just about what happens after we die. God has promised rewards to his followers here on Earth. But God's rewards are often not what we expect. God indeed provides for his children, but that's not a guarantee of worldly riches. In fact, what God offers us is better than anything this world could give us. What God has in store for you in his Church is amazing. I am praying for you that as you take the next steps in your journey, God will reveal more and more grace to you. Remember, it's not going to be easy, but it is going to be worth it. The blessings far outweigh the sacrifices. May you never look back. May you always remember the joy in discovering the treasure. And may you continue to abide in Christ and in his Church. So much adventure is waiting to be unearthed. Let's get digging.

About The Author

Keith Nester was raised in the home of a United Methodist Pastor. After pursuing his dream of playing music professionally, Keith sensed a call from God to enter the ministry. In 1995 at the age of 20, Keith became a Youth Pastor and Worship leader. His career in ministry would last for 22 years as Keith served in various capacities in several different churches. Most of Keith's ministry centered on youth, worship leading and preaching.

In 2017, after many years of prayer and study, Keith became convinced that the Roman Catholic Church was the Church founded by Jesus Christ, and contained the fullness of the Christian faith. In the spring of that year, Keith resigned his job at his church and began his official conversion into Roman Catholicism. On October 8th, 2017 Keith was received into the Church. His wife Estelle (who was raised Catholic but left the Church as a young adult) returned to the Church that day as well.

Keith and Estelle have three adult children. Keith and Estelle own and operate Cast of Thousands Photography in Marion, Iowa.

For more information, or to bring Keith to your parish or event, visit *keithnester.com*. Keith can also be found on YouTube at Keith Nester, on Instagram at *keithnestercatholic*, and on Facebook at *Keith Nester Catholic Speaker*

Printed in France by Amazon
Brétigny-sur-Orge, FR

16820778R00132